EARLY YEARS
ACTIVITY CHEST

Threes and under

British Library Cataloguing-in-Publication Data
A catalogue record for this book is available from the British Library.

ISBN 0 439 01760 2

ACKNOWLEDGEMENTS
The publishers gratefully acknowledge permission to reproduce the following copyright material:
Irene Yates for 'A letter to Grandma' © 2000, Irene Yates, previously unpublished.

Every effort has been made to trace copyright holders and the publishers apologize for any inadvertent omissions.

AUTHOR
Hannah Mortimer

EDITOR
Sally Gray

ASSISTANT EDITOR
Lesley Sudlow

SERIES DESIGNER
Lynne Joesbury

DESIGNER
Anna Oliwa

ILLUSTRATIONS
Kate Davies

COVER PHOTOGRAPH
Fiona Pragoff

Text © 2000 Hannah Mortimer
© 2000 Scholastic Ltd

Designed using Adobe Pagemaker
Published by Scholastic Ltd, Villiers House,
Clarendon Avenue, Leamington Spa, Warwickshire CV32 5PR
Printed by Alden Group Ltd, Oxford
Visit our website at www.scholastic.co.uk

3 4 5 6 7 8 9 0   2 3 4 5 6 7 8 9

CONTENTS

CONTENTS

Introduction

The aims of the series
This book forms part of a series that provides useful activities for filling pockets of time in a productive and enjoyable way. You will find a mixture of activities suitable for younger children up to and including the age of three, which help them to practise skills and enjoy experiences across all of the areas of early learning.

How to use this book
The six activity chapters each relate to one of the six areas of the Early Learning Goals and contain ten activities each. There are activities to encourage early personal, social and emotional development, communication, language and literacy skills, mathematical development,

knowledge and understanding of the world, physical development and creative development. The activities are timed and can be dipped into and used in a productive and useful way. Each activity is described using the same headings, with full details of what you will need, any preparation required, step-by-step instructions and advice on carrying out the activity. Differentiation is provided for younger and older children, ways of maintaining links with home and ideas for providing multicultural links are also given.

Very young children respond best to several short play activities with the chance to make their own choices in between. You can use the activity chapters to plan short activities ahead, or you can dip into the book when you find you have a few minutes to spare. Most of the activities require little preparation, and can therefore be used quickly and easily.

Remember that young children do not split their session into separate areas of activities or themes, and you will need to be flexible in the way you plan. Be ready to reassure and encourage the children when you are introducing new ideas, and balance this with familiarity and the chance for a child to repeat favourite activities.

How to use the photocopiable sheets
Very young children respond best to practical experiences rather than to recording on paper. There are twelve photocopiable sheets that can be used to support your practical play, and can also be used as a home link at the end of the session. You can make these visually interesting by photocopying onto brightly-coloured paper if appropriate, or duplicating to A3 size if a child would find it easier. A few of the sheets would also benefit from being photocopied onto thin card to make them into a more permanent record. Most of the sheets are illustrated to make them

attractive; some children might enjoy colouring these over with broad crayon or brush strokes, but they should not be expected to colour in carefully just yet.

Using a wide range of resources

The activities in this book make use of the wide range of materials and resources available in most early years settings. Very young children respond well to materials that they can handle and explore, and enjoy making links between their actions and the effects that these have on the materials. Be prepared to be flexible if the way the children respond to the materials suddenly presents new opportunities for learning. Use the photocopiable sheets as a starting point and a general idea and then 'go with the child' if this is going to enrich their early learning and experience.

Some of the activities need larger spaces. Make use of any indoor hall or outdoor playing areas for these, but be aware of the children's safety at all times. Young children are easily distracted and need close supervision outdoors. Floor areas need to be clean and suitable for lying and rolling on as well as walking and dancing on. Carpeted and cushioned areas are invaluable for sharing a song or a story, or for gathering in a circle. Use floor spaces and low tables which allow the adults to 'get down to the child's level' as far as possible.

Watch out for very young children who might still be at the stage of placing objects in their mouths and exploring them. This is a natural stage and one of the ways that they explore objects around them. Avoid small loose objects that might be swallowed, and gradually show the child that there are other ways of exploring new objects which are just as interesting and fun.

Links with home

Very young children react best to the flexibility which home-based learning can provide. Learn what you can from what works with the children in your care, and try to create an atmosphere for very early learning which has all the reassurance and familiarity of a family and home-based setting.

Each activity carries ideas to involve family and home with their child's learning, making your links with home a two-way partnership. Look for ways of involving families in your group setting and sharing their child's progress. Try to share the reasoning behind your activities as well as what you have been doing together.

Working with children under three

Adult to child ratios for children under three vary from 1:2 to 1:6 depending on the child's age, the kind of provision and whether parents can be contacted immediately. Your Local Authority or Early Years and Childcare Service will be able to inform you of the current regulations.

Each activity in this book suggests a possible group size and level of supervision. You will need to make your own judgements on this, based on your knowledge of the particular children in your group and the activity concerned.

Throughout this book, you will find many ideas for working with very young children. Keep the activities as home-like and flexible as possible. Allow for a repetition of favourite activities by following the children's interests. Sandwich short activities with periods of activity and free play so that interest and attention are not lost.

Use your own presence, reassurance and encouragement to hold the children's attention and to build their confidence as they try out new things. Make sure that you are aware of their safety, happiness and well-being at all times.

Planning for individual needs

Young children vary widely in their stages of development and the activities contain ideas for extension and support to enable you to plan for their individual needs. You will find this easiest if you try to 'tune in' to each child and follow what fascinates and motivates them most. By playing alongside them, you can encourage each child in what they can nearly do now, gradually showing them new ways of making links in their thinking, their talking and their play. Above all, talk to the children about what they are doing, providing the simple words that link language to what they are doing.

Because all children aged three and under are playing at an early stage of their development, it is not difficult to meet any special educational needs inclusively within your setting. Use the support ideas in the chapters, making them appropriate for each child's age and stage. Plan your activities ahead, but do not worry if your activities for very young children do not always go to plan! Always be ready to change an activity if you need to hold the children's interest; it is always best to finish while the children are still enjoying it!

All of the activities in this book suggest an ideal number of children for the group. Because children's needs change so greatly from the age of one to three, the group sizes given have been aimed at an average group of two- to three-year-olds. You might be able to organize the activities in slightly larger groups for three-year-olds and you would need individual attention for children as young as one. Get to know the children and their needs individually and then decide on the adult ratio that is going to work best for each activity. Again, 'flexibility' is the key – keep the children's individual needs at the heart of your planning. Some of the activities suggest working with only two or three children at a time. This becomes easiest if you have one adult organizing the activity with the children in turns, and the others supervising and supporting the play and personal needs of the rest of the group.

Each child has a right to develop and learn in a society without prejudice or discrimination. Equal opportunities must be a central concern to your setting and arise from the whole group's attitudes and belief in what it is trying to achieve. Each child also needs to feel confident and valued in your setting. Your sessions might be their first experience of meeting other children and behaving and playing within a social group. Remember how important it is to encourage children's positive self-esteem, and keep positive encouragement, continual reassurance and clear information about behaviour at the heart of your management and teaching. The child who tries something new and meets success becomes more confident and is more likely to try again.

Learning in a multicultural world

Many of the activities have suggestions for multicultural links. Sometimes you will be able to make use of the direct experiences of the children and families who attend your group or to involve members of your local community in your setting. This provides another useful way of making links to homes, families and cultures. For others, you will need to look for opportunities of introducing other cultures to the children so that you can celebrate the wide variety of cultures and beliefs within society. The multicultural activity ideas will provide you with some starting points.

This chapter provides ten activities for encouraging personal, social and emotional development in very young children. The children are encouraged to make friends and play co-operatively with each other. Throughout, they are stimulated to think about feelings and helping each other, and there is an opportunity to celebrate a festival together.

Personal, social and emotional development

GROUP SIZE
Whole group, with one adult per four children.

TIMING
Ten minutes.

FEELING MUSICAL

Learning objective
To respond to music with a range of feelings and movement.

What you need
A large empty space; cassette player and six pieces of music on cassette. Provide a range of interesting and contrasting music styles, some fast or exciting, others calm and gentle!

Preparation
Select the pieces of music that you are going to play (about two minutes of each). Set the tapes to the right place to start.

HOME LINKS
Use your newsletter or group notice-board to make suggestions of different music that the children might like to listen to at home, or encourage children to bring in their favourites.

What to do
Take your children to the large space and explain that you are going to listen and move to some different types of music. Play your first tape and encourage the adults to begin to move as unselfconsciously as possible. This becomes much easier if each adult partners a child to 'get each other going'.

Move freely to the music, copying the smooth, jumpy or striding sounds that you hear. Stop after a minute or two, wait for the children to settle, and then move on to the next piece of music.

Support
Self-conscious adults can be supported by a child; younger children by a confident adult!

MULTICULTURAL LINKS
Select a range of music from a variety of cultures. Look for firm rhythms, new melodies and sounds, and music with distinctive character and atmosphere.

Extension
Talk to the older children about the movements that they are making. Ask them what the music 'told' them to do. Pause the tape and invite them to show the other children. Encourage new and different ideas.

GROUP SIZE
Six children.

TIMING
Ten minutes.

HOME LINKS
Ask for help to reinforce 'looking' skills by suggesting things to look out for on the children's journey to and from your group.

LOOKING TOGETHER

Learning objective
To develop looking skills and gain respect for other children.

What you need
Eighteen white cards (A5 size); coloured pens.

Preparation
Draw one large coloured circle on six separate cards – two red, two blue and two yellow. Draw pictures on six more cards, for example, two with a tractor on; two with a cat; two with a tree. Draw a set of objects on the six remaining cards, for example, two with one ladybird on; two with two ladybirds on, and two with three ladybirds on. Mix up the cards within each set.

What to do
Gather the children together in a circle. Tell them that they are going to play a game about looking. What can they see around them? Give each child a card, starting with the colour cards. Ask each child to hold their card and look at it. Can they see a colour?

Start with a confident child and explain that someone else has the same colour on their card as them. Hold the child's hand and walk around the inside of the circle asking each child to show their card. Help the children to compare and contrast their cards until a partner with the same colour card is found. Show all of the children the colour and decide what it is called. Move the children with the same colour cards so that the two partners sit together. Repeat for the other two pairs so that each child is sitting next to their partner. Encourage them to hold hands with their partner and rock backwards and forwards for the song, 'Row, Row, Row Your Boat' from *This Little Puffin...* compiled by Elizabeth Matterson (Puffin).

Return to your circle and repeat the game with the picture cards, and then the cards with the sets of objects. Between each game, sing a verse of the song so that the children can enjoy time with their new partner.

Support
Younger children will need your help to count their set or name their colour. Help them to look carefully at the two cards together to decide whether they are the same or different.

Extension
Ask older children to help you to make the matching cards. Draw the first one in each set and help them to copy them.

GROUP SIZE
Two children at a
time.

TIMING
Five minutes (just
before home-time).

ALL BY MYSELF

Learning objective
To develop early dressing skills.

What you need
Each child's coat hanging up; a whistling party blower which extends;
coloured stickers (optional).

What to do
Invite two of your children, who have not yet learned to put on their
coats, to join you for five minutes before home-time. Find a quiet space
near to the coat hooks where you will not disturb the other children.
Explain that you are going to help them learn how to put on their coats
and, when they can do it, you will blow your funny whistle. Show them
first to make sure it does not frighten them.

First, ascertain how much of the task each child can do on their own.
Can they reach their own coats from the hooks? As each child manages,
blow your whistle in triumph and praise them warmly. Can they hold
their coat up by the inside neck? Put a sticker there if it is difficult to
locate. Teach each child, arm-by-arm, to put their sleeves on. Give plenty
of praise at each step. Finally, help them shrug their coat up to their
shoulders. Place any zip into its foot and encourage the child to pull it up
with a final whistle blow.

As you complete this activity, you will have noticed what each child
can do unaided or with help. Make a note of where your help is still
needed. Next time you do this activity, only help with those parts of the
task. Continue to praise warmly and keep the activity fun until the child
is able to do it alone.

Support
Place your hand gently over the child's hand to help them through difficult
parts of the task.

Extension
Use a similar approach to break down the tasks of putting on shoes
correctly, or turning a coat 'outside-in' and so on.

HOME LINKS
Keep parents and
carers in touch with
their child's progress
and encourage
them to provide
only as much help
as is absolutely
necessary, praising
all efforts warmly.
Copy the
photocopiable
sheet on page 72
and send the special
certificate home
when their child has
put on their coat
(or achieved
something else) 'all
by myself'.

GROUP SIZE
Whole group
(children and
adults).

TIMING
Five to ten minutes
(at the beginning of
a session).

PLANNING AHEAD

Learning objective
To make simple choices and plans in independent play.

What you need
A train whistle; coloured cards in the shape of engines and trucks – (a train and a truck shape for each child); a bold, black felt-tipped pen.

Preparation
Lay out all your planned activities for the session.

What to do
Gather all the children and adults together in a long line (train style). Ask each person to hold onto the person in front of them around their waist. Tell the children that you are going on a pretend train journey around the room to see what is happening today. Lead the train, slowly shuffling along with a 'puff puff puff' as you move to the first activity. Blow your whistle to stop the train.

In a theatrical style, tell the children what the first activity has in store for them. Move around to the next activity, and halt your train again. Choose up to six activities to show to the children.

Now come back to your carpeted area and break into small groups of three or four children to each adult. Talk to the children about what they have seen as they moved around the room.

Ask each child to think about which activity they would like to do first. Draw a simple representation of that activity on an engine shape and let the child place it on the floor in front of them. Then ask each child what they would like to do next. Draw that on a truck shape and help the child place it behind the engine. Let that child go off to start playing, encouraging them to stick to the plan on their shapes.

Support
Limit the idea to one activity at a time for very young children.

Extension
Older children could cope with planning three or four activities and will need more than one 'truck'. Display the children's engines and trucks and encourage them to refer back to them. Later, talk about how their plans worked out. Ask, 'Did you do the activities in the correct order? What did you enjoy best? What will you do tomorrow?'.

HOME LINKS
Copy the
photocopiable sheet
on page 73 and
provide the children
with a simple
pictorial diary to fill
in together. Let
them take them
home to show their
parents and carers
what special
activities they have
done that week.

ALL'S FAIR

Learning objective
To take turns and share freely.

What you need
Sponge cube (10cm); red, blue and yellow paint or felt-tipped pens; large construction bricks in the same three colours (the bricks should piece together easily).

Preparation
Make a giant dice out of a cube of sponge and use paint or coloured pens to paint opposite sides red, blue or yellow.

What to do
This is a non-competitive game where each 'turn' has a result and everyone can share the end product! Invite four children to sit with you in a small circle on a mat. Take it in turns around the circle to roll the dice towards the centre of the circle. When it has stopped, encourage everyone to look at the colour facing uppermost. Encourage the children to name the colour if they can, providing the correct name yourself if necessary. Now pass the box of bricks to the child who has just thrown. Can they find a brick of the same colour? If you need to, hold different bricks against the dice so the children can make comparisons. Ask them to place their brick in front of them on the floor. Praise the children who are waiting patiently and 'helping'.

Continue around the circle throwing the dice until everyone has four bricks. Now invite each child to fit their own four bricks together to make a tower. How can you make a bigger model all together? Undo your bricks, then take it in turns to piece your bricks all together to make an even higher tower and praise the children for sharing their bricks together.

Support
For very young children, start with only two children in the group and gradually increase the number.

Extension
Play the game with six different colours, one on each side of the dice.

SOFTLY, SOFTLY

Learning objective
To concentrate while listening.

What you need
An extra adult helper; a set of jingle bells for each child.

What to do
Gather the children around and talk about listening. Encourage them to listen while you stamp your feet – what can they hear? Now walk along very quietly – can they still hear anything? Introduce the words 'loudly' and 'softly'. Can the children clap their hands *loudly*? Now can they clap their hands *softly*? Can they shout *loudly*? Now can they whisper very, very *softly*?

Invite the children to hold their hands over their eyes as you walk around, to see if they can hear you. Few of them will in fact cover their eyes completely and some will not wish to – this is fine at this stage! Stamp or tiptoe around them and ask the children if you are walking loudly or softly. Now explain that you would like the children to walk around you very softly while you close your eyes! Ask your helper to watch the children and encourage them with actions. Praise their quietness, and tell them how softly they are walking.

Give each child a set of jingle bells. Encourage them to play them loudly and then to try playing them softly. Challenge the children to have another turn at walking around you softly, but this time carrying some jingle bells! Can they still walk very, very softly? Cover your eyes again as your helper silently encourages the children. Praise their attempts without criticism. Vary the game by using other instruments.

Support
Younger children might need a helper to lead them by the hand. Ask the helper to emphasize the words *loud* and *soft* as appropriate.

Extension
Let older children take a turn as a listener.

GROUP SIZE
Two children.

TIMING
Five minutes.

BEING FRIENDS

Learning objective
To play alongside another child.

What you need
A selection of toys suitable for two children to play with co-operatively (such as two train sets and a track, farm animals and farmyard, or the home corner.)

What to do
Invite an older or fairly confident child to play with the toys. Ask if they would mind if you and another child watched. Invite a shy or a younger child to come and watch with you. Stay close to them and talk gently as you watch the child play. Use your words as a running commentary about what is going on – 'Can you see Jonathan has the train now? I wonder if he's going to make a tunnel?'. Pass the second child their own set of the toys and talk gently as you encourage them to play. Look for opportunities to draw the children's attention to each other. For example, 'Jonathan is looking for a cup; can you pass him one of yours?'. By staying beside the children, you will be encouraging them to concentrate and remain interested for longer. You will also be encouraging them to begin to watch what the other is doing. Play between the children is most likely to start when you are playing too.

Show the children how to play co-operatively, providing ideas for making the game more enjoyable but always taking the lead from them if they produce their own ideas. Step back once co-operation begins to develop. This may take the younger children several sessions with your presence and encouragement.

Support
This activity is particularly suitable for a very young child who is not used to playing with other children. It is also useful for a shy child or a new starter who has not yet developed the confidence to mix socially with other children.

Extension
Use this activity to encourage older or more confident children to involve the shyer child in their play.

HOME LINKS
Encourage parents and carers to invite 'friends' round to play at home. Suggest that they stay close to encourage the children to play together.

GROUP SIZE
Whole group.

TIMING
Ten minutes.

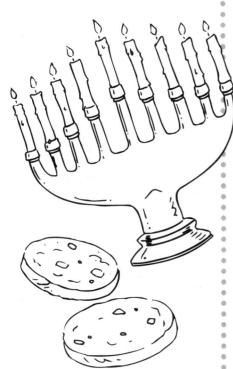

FESTIVAL FEAST

Learning objective
To respond to a cultural and religious event.

What you need
Potato latkes or potato cakes (see Preparation below), a menorah (a branched candlestick) with pretend candles made from cardboard and crêpe paper 'flames'. In this particular activity, the Jewish festival of light, Hanukkah, is being celebrated. You could equally celebrate the Christian festivals of Christmas or Harvest, the Muslim festival of Eid-ul-Fitr, the Hindu festival of Divali or the Chinese New Year.

Preparation
Make the latkes at home before the session. For 25 latkes you will need: 1kg potatoes; 500g finely grated onions; 2 eggs; 500g plain flour; pepper, salt and frying oil. Peel and grate the potatoes and rinse away the starch. Mix the ingredients together and shape into 25 oval cakes. Fry gently on both sides and store with greaseproof paper between layers. If possible, warm them up just before the activity.

What to do
This activity will make most sense to the children if it forms part of a wider topic which celebrates Hanukkah. Gather the children together and show them the menorah with its eight candleholders. Involve any children who celebrate Hanukkah to talk about what they will be doing at home. Tell the children that the candles show us that light makes the darkness go away and it reminds us of the need to tell the truth. Ask, 'Who knows what 'telling the truth' means? What does 'telling a lie' mean?'. Encourage the children to think of examples. Share out the latkes and tell the children that this is one of the special foods that people might eat at Hanukkah.

Support
Let younger children sit close to an adult so that they can talk together about what is happening.

HOME LINKS
Encourage families to tell you about festivals that they celebrate so that you can adapt this activity to include everyone.

MULTICULTURAL LINKS
Try to involve family members who celebrate each festival to join you. Invite them to show the children some of the special things that they use or eat during their festival.

Extension
Invite older children to help you make the menorah by forming eight Plasticine candleholders and joining them to one stand.

GROUP SIZE
Three or four
children at a time.

TIMING
Five minutes (at the
beginning of the
session).

HOME LINKS
Give the cuddly toys
something to take
home with them at
the end of the
session, such as a
picture or a model
that the children
have painted or
made for them.

CUDDLIES AND COMFORTERS

Learning objective
To develop simple words for feelings and to gain confidence.

What you need
Each child and adult needs their own favourite cuddly toy or comforter.

What to do
Invite the children and their 'cuddlies' to come and sit with you on the mat. Introduce your own toy and talk about when you were little, such as how you would cuddle your toy in bed or when you were poorly or frightened. Tell them how you also liked to take it with you when you went anywhere new, such as nursery.

Invite the children to tell you the name of their 'cuddlies'. Ask, 'When do you like to be with your cuddly toy? Who likes to cuddle their toy when they feel sad? How does your cuddly toy make you feel? Does anyone know what 'lonely' means? Who likes to cuddle their toy when they feel lonely?'. Invite the children to make their 'cuddlies' say 'hello' to each other and sing a song together that the 'cuddlies' can join in.

Now suggest that the children take their 'cuddlies' around your group and show them all of the activities. Suggest a quiet area where the 'cuddlies' can go when the children want to be busy.

Support
Suggest that very young children continue to bring a cuddly toy to your group to help them settle in. Discourage young children from using a dummy in nursery as this will get in the way of language development. However, you could always have a special jar for it to sit in!

Extension
Encourage older children to talk about things that make them happy or sad. Ask them to suggest why a cuddly toy can help.

GROUP SIZE
Two or three children at a time (as the need arises).

TIMING
Five minutes.

FEELING BETTER

Learning objective
To develop a sensitivity to other children's needs and feelings.

What to do
The most effective time to teach very young children about how to deal with feelings is as those feelings arise. This is an activity for making the most of those moments.

Whenever you are comforting a child, lead them to a comfortable chair and begin to make them feel better. Ask one or two children to help you. 'Why do you think Tara is crying? Shall we ask her? Did we see what happened? How do you think she's feeling now? Is that right, Tara? How can we make Tara feel better? Shall we try?'

Use the opportunity to talk together about sad feelings and making them better. Think about things that make the children feel happy again and try them out together. Talk about hurting, and being kind. Always encourage and help the children to say sorry, even if you are leading them gently by the hand and saying it for them. Once 'Tara' has calmed down, try to use the group of children to distract her so that she can begin to play more happily again.

Support
Very young children will need you to stay close as they settle. They might find it hard to see how the other child is feeling, but they should be able to think of ways to make them feel better, such as a hug.

Extension
Older children need encouragement to think about how another child is feeling. They may need constant reminders about this until they are about five or six years old.

HOME LINKS
Tell parents and carers about your group's policy for encouraging the children to be kind to each other.

MULTICULTURAL LINKS
Create the right environment for encouraging equal opportunities, respect and mutual understanding. You might find the booklet *Equal Chances: Eliminating discrimination and ensuring equality in pre-school* (Pre-school Learning Alliance) a useful addition to your group's library.

In this chapter, you will find ten short activities to support early learning in communication, language and literacy. The broad range of activities includes ideas for developing thinking and speaking skills, early imaginative play, mark- making and exploring stories and books as well as encouraging early recognition of rhythm and rhyme in language.

GROUP SIZE
Three children.

TIMING
Five minutes.

Communication, language and literacy

ALL ABOUT ME

Learning objective
To listen in a small group and talk about experiences.

What you need
A hand-held plastic mirror.

What to do
Sit together in a comfortable area. Introduce the activity by telling the children that you are each going to talk 'all about me'. Start by holding up the mirror yourself and asking, 'What do I see?'. Describe your hair,

eyes, smile and what you are wearing. Pass the mirror around to each child in turn, asking them what they see. Encourage the child with the mirror to talk and the others to listen. Now pass the mirror around again and encourage the child holding it to say something that they like doing. Later, ask about home, families and what they like to eat. All the time, encourage the mirror-holder to talk and the others to listen.

Draw the activity together by suggesting that each child is both different and special. Ask, 'How are each one of you *special* today? Who is the tallest? Who is wearing red? How are you all the *same* today? Who has hair the same length? Who has clothes the same colour? Who is the same age?'.

Finish by telling each child in turn why you think they are special and talk about all the things that they have learned to do in your group. Praise the children for talking and listening to each other so well, and for being friendly to each other.

Support
Younger children will need you to ask direct questions, and even to provide choices such as, 'Is your hair long or short?'. If necessary, provide concrete examples such as, 'Is your hair *long* like Alice's, or *short* like Tariq's?'.

Extension
Encourage older children to describe themselves in detail and to make comparisons with each other. Invite them to say one thing that they like about each of the other children.

HOME LINKS
Ask parents and carers to help their child choose their favourite photograph of themselves and bring it in to share with the other children. Why do they like that photograph best?

MULTICULTURAL LINKS
Celebrate multicultural differences and make each child feel special.

TOUCH AND FEEL

Learning objective
To enjoy books and handle them carefully.

What you need
A collection of ten or more touch-and-feel books (include books made from interesting textures, books with movable characters, books with textured inserts, lift-the-flap texture books and pop-up books); low shelves or a table to display the books on; comfortable floor cushions.

Preparation
Contact your local library to enquire about their collection of sensory books for young children. Many libraries now keep a special list of books that encourage touching, feeling and early talking.

What to do
Arrange four or five books on your shelves or table, so that the children are not overwhelmed by choice. Invite two or three children to join you on the cushions, asking that each child chooses a book to bring to you.

Introduce each book to the children, holding their attention all the time. Show them how to lift the flaps gently, feel the textures or move the characters. Give each child a job to do to keep them fully involved. Talk about the textures, introducing new words to describe how the pages feel. Talk together about the pictures and what is happening. Encourage the children to think about what might happen next. Praise their turn taking as they wait until it is time to share the book that they have chosen. Encourage them to be gentle as they handle the books and turn the pages. Finish before the children lose interest, returning to a new selection of books at the next session.

Support
Work with younger children individually.

Extension
Include standard picture books in your collection, encouraging the children to talk in more detail about what is going on and why they have chosen that book.

HOW DO YOU DO?

Learning objective
To begin to associate sounds with patterns in rhymes.

What you need
A large pair of heavy working boots.

What to do
Gather the children in a circle, sitting on the floor. Tell them that you are going to put on your large boots and make your feet march all around the circle. Ask them to sit still and listen to the noise you make. Put on your boots and stamp around the outside of the circle, with a heavy 'one, two' rhythm. Can the children count 'one, two' as you march? Parade around the circle again as you all chant 'one, two, one, two'. Let the children stand up and copy you as you all march around, chanting together.

Now come back to your circle and kneel together, facing the centre. Ask the children to copy you as you alternate your hands on the floor, one, two, one, two. Teach the children this chant, to the rhythm of all your hand beats on the floor:

'One, two, how do you do?
I'm very well, and how are you?'

Repeat the chant together, once for each child, as you nod your head to each child in turn and shake hands to greet them. Finish with the children following you in a march around the room, chanting the rhyme to anyone else in the room as you meet them. Keep a strong beat going with your boots.

Support
Place very young children next to you in the circle, so that you can help them hand-over-hand. You may need to lead them by the hand during the march, as they find it hard to follow 'behind'. The children may not be able to keep a beat yet – this is fine. They are still hearing the rhythm of your words and linking it to the stamp of your feet.

Extension
Invite older children to say the second line of the rhyme on their own, in response to your first line. Choose one or two of the children to beat a percussion instrument when you enjoy your final march around the room.

GROUP SIZE
Three or four
children.

TIMING
Ten minutes.

PUPPET PLAY

Learning objective
To take part in puppet role-play with confidence.

What you need
A box; some simple glove puppets, at least one for each child; a musical cassette suitable for dancing to (a modern release or perhaps Tchaikovsky's *Nutcracker Suite*); cassette recorder.

Preparation
Place your puppets in a box and set your music up ready to play.

HOME LINKS
Give each child a
copy of the
photocopiable sheet
on page 74 to take
home. It contains
ideas for puppet
play such as puppet
talk on toy
telephones, puppet
story-time, a puppet
play using a box as
the stage and
making simple sock
puppets with
button eyes.

What to do
Gather the children together on the floor and show them the box of puppets. Explore them together, trying the puppets on and making them speak and dance. Ask each child to choose a puppet for a game of musical bumps. If the children find it hard to share, take it in turns and swap puppets each time.

Play the music and invite the children to make their puppets dance. When the music stops, ask them to 'bump' their puppets to the floor. After a few turns, encourage the children to make their puppets play 'musical statues'. When the music stops, the children have to try to keep the puppets absolutely still until the music starts again. Keep this game non-competitive; no one should be 'out' and all of the puppets should be praised for joining in well.

As the game progresses, encourage the children to speak to their puppets and give them names. Ask the children for more ideas of how the puppets can play together.

Finish by 'coming out of role'. Talk to the children again, help them to remove their puppets and put them away for another time.

MULTICULTURAL LINKS
Look out for
puppets that reflect
a multicultural
theme such as
Chinese dragons,
multicultural
costumes or
favourite story
characters from
around the world.

Support
Some younger children are frightened of puppets because they seem to move in an unpredictable way. Try the activity with teddy bears, if this seems less threatening.

Extension
Encourage older children to speak for their puppets and think imaginatively about what their puppets might do.

GROUP SIZE
One or two
children at a time.

TIMING
Five minutes.

HOME LINKS
Empty the post-box
at home time so
that any letters to
family members can
be delivered. Ask
the child to 'read'
the message to
parents and carers,
helping out if
necessary by
reading the notes
that you made on
the reverse side. At
the next session,
invite parents and
carers to post a
simple message to
their child. Look at
the writing together
and read out the
messages to them.

POST IT

Learning objective
To use mark-making and symbols to represent a message.

What you need
The story on the photocopiable sheet on page 69; a large cardboard box; red paint; small pieces of paper in different shapes; mark-making implements suitable for younger children (stubby crayons, washable felt-tipped pens, soft pencils).

Preparation
Cut a posting hole in your cardboard box and paint it red to look like a post-box. Arrange the paper and writing implements on a table with chairs around.

What to do
Encourage one or two children to join you in the story corner and read them the story on the photocopiable sheet on page 69. Now move to the table and explain that you are going to play at writing letters, too. Ask, 'Who would you like to write to? What would you like to say?'. Help the children to write their pretend letters by choosing a piece of paper and a writing implement and making marks to represent writing. As you 'write', talk about the message that you are sending. Talk about all the different messages that letters can be used for. Write the child's name, a note to say what the child was communicating and who the message was for on the reverse of the letter. When the letter is finished, show each child how to fold and post their letter into the post-box.

Support
Encourage younger children to make any marks they can. Show them how to hold the crayon so that it makes a mark and use hand-over-hand to help them fold their letter.

Extension
Help older children to position their crayon properly in their hand. Encourage them to write their name, providing feint letters for them to copy over if necessary.

GROUP SIZE
Three or four
children.

TIMING
Five to ten minutes.

HOME LINKS
Consolidate this
work by sending
home picture
sheets with
drawings of the ten
objects and their
names for children
to talk about with
their families.

**MULTICULTURAL
LINKS**
Ask parents and
carers to help you
gather a collection
of objects for
multicultural
themes. Take time
to remember their
labels and
pronunciations and
to find out their
functions.

NAME IT!

Learning objective
To use and understand a growing vocabulary.

What you need
A colourful box made to look like a treasure chest with ten objects inside. Rotate the objects so that there is a different selection for each session.

Preparation
Select your objects, perhaps linked to your current topic, such as zoo animals (toy giraffe, chimpanzee, lemur and so on); things that we use at home (kettle, jug, fork and so on). Keep a balance between familiar items and more unusual objects to stretch the imagination and memory.

What to do
When you have a few minutes between activities, reach for the treasure chest. Gather the children around, and encourage them to look carefully as you see what is in the box today. Invite the children to take turns to lift out and talk about an object. What is it called? What is it used for? Pass each object around so that everybody has a chance to look at it and feel it. Now place the objects back in the box and invite the children to say the names of the objects as you lift each one out. Praise the children for how well they have remembered.

Support
Younger children will benefit by working with older children and hearing the answers that they give. Start with a few familiar objects and keep any objects that are difficult to name in the box for another time. Revisit objects from time to time to increase confidence and aid memory. For children with language difficulties, keep a note of their progress and repeat the activity on a one-to-one basis with them.

Extension
Make the selection more challenging for older children. If you are collecting objects within a theme, invite the children to gather them with you.

HIGH AND LOW

Learning objective
To develop an understanding of abstract vocabulary.

What you need
A favourite teddy bear or toy; at least one other adult helper.

Preparation
Think of a few safe hiding places for your toy.

What to do
Gather the children together and teach them these actions. When you say 'hands *high*', all raise your arms high above your heads. When you say 'hands *low*', all lower your arms to the floor. Practise this a few times.

Now tell the children that you are going to play a hiding game. You will ask your helper to go out of the room while you hide the teddy somewhere for her to find. Explain to the children that the bear can be hidden 'up

high' or 'down *low*'. Encourage the children to give you ideas and then hide the teddy so that it is still visible to the searcher. Share the children's excitement as you call your helper back in, and encourage the children to do their very best not to give the secret away. The helper should ask the children, 'Is it *high* or *low*?'. Encourage the children to answer and cheer when the teddy is found.

Invite any of the children to take a turn. Ask your helper to lead them out of the room and provide constant encouragement when the child returns to search. Keep emphasizing the key words *high* and *low*. Continue until you have to stop, or until all those who want to have had a go.

Support
Give younger children an extra clue by all holding your arms *high* or *low* to help them know where to look.

Extension
Older children can hide the toy or search on their own, but they will still need a helper to take them out the room. Offer three options – *high*, *low* or *in the middle*.

STORY BOX

Learning objective
To listen and respond to stories.

What you need
A cardboard box, coloured brightly with a character from your favourite picture book depicted on the outside. Put props to go with your picture book inside the box.

Preparation
Story boxes can be used as long-term resources for your group. Involve the children in your preparation as part of this project. Talk with the children and decide on your favourite picture book together, such as *Dear Zoo* by Rod Campbell (Puffin). Tell the children that you would like to fill the story box with as many of the creatures or objects as you can from the book. Some children will volunteer to bring a toy in for you to borrow. You might collect several story boxes each term.

What to do
Gather the children together and tell them that it is 'Story box' time. Choose the story that you are going to talk about, and start to read through the book, inviting the children to turn the page or lift the flaps. At each page, pause to encourage a child to find the right prop from the story box and make it act out the story. You will often find that the children get very involved and make suggestions for new props, or offer to bring something in, or make it. Involve them as much as possible. Repeat the story at their request.

Support
Give younger children one of your props to hold, and involve them closely in looking at the pictures or lifting the flaps.

Extension
Involve older children in preparing your story box project, and follow through their ideas by helping them to create more props for the box.

HICKORY DICKORY

Learning objective
To listen and respond to nursery rhymes.

What to do
Gather the children in a circle to sing the familiar nursery rhyme, 'Hickory Dickory Dock':

Hickory Dickory Dock,
The mouse ran up the clock;
The clock struck One,
The mouse ran down,
Hickory Dickory Dock!

As you sing, use your fingers to make a 'mouse' running up your arm, clap your hands once for the 'one', and then make your fingers run down again. Now suggest that you make up some other verses for the song. Perhaps the clock could strike two? Sing the rhyme again, this time changing the third line.

'The clock struck Two, the mouse went COO!'

Continue with a third and fourth verse, looking for words which sound like 'three' and 'four'. Emphasize the sounds so that the children can hear the similarity of the rhymes.

'The clock struck Three, the mouse went TEE HEE!'
'The clock struck Four, the mouse went ROAR!'

Encourage the children to contribute ideas and each time the clock 'strikes', all pause to clap your hands the appropriate number of times, counting steadily and clearly as you go.

Support
Sit younger children beside you so that you can help them with the clapping.

Extension
Ask older children to contribute ideas for the rhyming words. Accept their ideas and try them out to see whether they fit to the tune. The children are not likely to produce their own rhyming words yet, but they may recognize when a rhyme you give them is correct. Take the rhyme up to six or beyond for children who are skilled in counting.

OUR BOOK

Learning objective
To make up a story and understand how books are organized.

What you need
A scrapbook made of three A3 sheets of coloured sugar paper, folded into a book and bound with wool (this will make an A4-size book of 12 pages); sheets of white paper; glue; used children's magazines or catalogues; crayons or felt-tipped pens; safety nursery scissors; a black felt-tipped pen.

Preparation
Put all of your materials out on a table with chairs around it.

What to do
This is an activity to return to in a spare five minutes. Tell the children that you are going to make a story-book together. Show them your scrapbook and use the correct vocabulary to talk about the *pages*, the *front* and the *back* of the book.

During the first session, encourage the children to think about what your book will be called. They might like to look through some of the magazines for ideas, or think of an idea themselves. Choose a good title together and write it for them in bold lettering on the front. Let the children choose or help them to draw an appropriate picture for the front. Help them to cut it out and glue it on.

In later sessions, take the story forward by asking the children for ideas. For each page, choose a picture or encourage the children to help you draw an illustration to cut out and glue in together. Use the children's words to write down what happens in the picture. When the book is finished, share it with the children and place it in your book corner for everybody to look at.

Support
Help younger children with the cutting and sticking. Try to offer only as much help as is needed, so that the children are gradually building up these skills themselves.

Extension
Encourage older children to begin to think and plan ahead. Talk together about the beginning, the middle and the end of their story so that they know the plan before they begin collecting pictures.

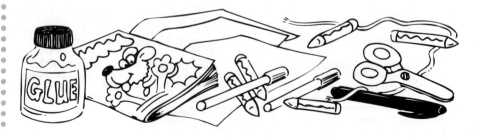

In this chapter, there are ten activities to support and encourage young children's understanding of mathematics. There are practical activities for exploring pattern, capacity and shape as well as motivating games to reinforce mathematical vocabulary and develop counting and number recognition skills.

Mathematical development

GROUP SIZE
Six to eight children.

TIMING
Five minutes.

ONE, TWO, THREE

Learning objective
To become familiar with a simple counting rhyme.

Preparation
Make yourself familiar with the rhyme on the photocopiable sheet on page 70.

What to do
Gather the children around and teach them the simple rhyme, 'One, two, three, look at me!' on the photocopiable sheet on page 70. Start by teaching the children the chorus, encouraging them to repeat each line at a time after you.

Introduce the verses, repeating the chorus between each one. Say the rhyme through two or three times together, and teach the children the actions to go with the words. At this stage, you may find that the children can perform the actions or the words, but not both of them together. That is fine, the important teaching point is to encourage three claps to the words 'one, two, three'.

Support
Younger children may be able to remember the chorus, but not the whole rhyme. Hold your hands gently over theirs to encourage three claps to the words 'one, two, three'.

Extension
Encourage older children to manage words and actions together. Suggest that the children think of different ways to repeat the 'one, two, three' rhythm, such as nodding their heads, tapping their knees or tapping their feet.

HOME LINKS
Copy the rhyme on the photocopiable sheet on page 70 for each child and encourage them to take it home and teach it to their families.

GROUP SIZE
Three or four children.

TIMING
Five minutes.

WATER PATTERNS

Learning objective
To recognize and develop patterns.

What you need
A warm, sunny day; a safe, paved area; flour; squeezy paint; glitter.

Preparation
Collect tubs (the size of a small bucket or ice-cream container) and part-fill with water and thick, stubby paintbrushes.

What to do
Take the children outside and show them how you can use your paintbrush to make water patterns and blobs on the paving. Share their surprise as the water slowly evaporates and talk about how the heat of the sun dries wet things. Encourage the children to experiment for a minute or two. Now paint a simple pattern and invite the children to keep it wet by painting over it as soon as it begins to dry. If the weather is not too hot, encourage the children to carry on the pattern which you have started, since it will not evaporate so quickly.

Continue with this theme at other spare moments. Make some thick but sloppy flour paste (one part flour to just over one part water), colour it with some squeezy paint and add some glitter. Place a thin layer over the bottom of a tray. Trace and copy each other's patterns, using fingertips. On a colder day, breathe on a sheet of glass and make patterns with your fingers. If you have a dry sand tray or sandpit, trace patterns in the surface.

Support
Younger children will find it easier to copy your movements rather than the pattern you are making. Make broad straight brushstrokes and encourage them to copy. Try making dabs, spiky movements and smooth circular movements for the children to copy.

Extension
Encourage older children to continue linear patterns and to create their own patterns for you to copy.

HOME LINKS

Make simple greetings cards by painting the front of the cards with thickened paint and then dragging combs across in wavy patterns. Let the children take them home.

MULTICULTURAL LINKS

Bring in examples of fabrics from around the world. Talk about the patterns and colours. Provide the children with paints in similar colours and invite them to express the colours and patterns that they have seen through a bright painting.

GROUP SIZE
Two children.

TIMING
Five minutes.

MORE AND MORE!

Learning objective
To use and understand simple words about quantity.

What you need
About twenty of one kind of object (small cars, animals or bricks) or alternatively use smooth pebbles (easy to handle but too large to be swallowed).

Preparation
Place a pile of your chosen objects in the middle of a table so that you can all stand around it and reach the pile.

What to do
Invite two children to come and see your collection of objects. Tell them that you are going to try to share them out. Smiling, give one to each child, and draw the rest towards yourself. 'There! Have we all got the *same* number?'. Share the joke as you talk about having *more*. Push most of your objects to one child, 'Who has *more* now?'. Give the remaining child most of the objects, keeping back only one for yourself. 'Now both of you have *more* than me!'. Encourage the children to share the objects out between the three of you. At this stage, you will be doing this by sight rather than by counting. Keep asking them, 'Who has *more* now? Are they the *same* yet?'. Encourage the children to co-operate as they work out how to solve the problem. Praise them warmly for succeeding, even if you have had to lend a helping hand at the last moment.

Support
Younger children, or those still developing abstract language, might need to watch this activity a few times until they have understood the meaning of the words *more* and *same*. Look for opportunities throughout the session to emphasize these words in order to help the children to generalize the meanings of them.

Extension
Invite older children to think of other ways to work out *same* and *more*, perhaps by counting or by lining the objects up together and using one-to-one correspondence.

HOME LINKS
Suggest to parents and carers that they give their child the opportunity to share out the biscuits or crisps at home. Explain that they are learning about *same*, *more* and *sharing out*.

GROUP SIZE
Three or four children.

TIMING
Ten minutes.

CIRCLES

Learning objective
To recognize and describe a simple shape.

What you need
A table; white paper plates; old food magazines; nursery safety scissors; glue.

Preparation
Arrange your materials on a table.

What to do
Gather the children around you and hold up one of the paper plates. Does anyone know what *shape* it is? Talk about *circles* and *round shapes*. Give each child one of the paper plates to hold. Ask the children if they can see anything else which is a *circle* shape in the room. As they call out suggestions, travel around the room together and hold up your plates to the object named to see if it looks like a circle. Look for large and small circle shapes.

Now come back to the table and suggest that the children find a favourite dinner to go on their round plate. Help them to find pictures of food from the magazines to cut out and stick onto their plate to make a 'dinner'.

Support
Younger children will find the searching part difficult. Provide some brightly-coloured cardboard circles, squares and triangles so that the children can make direct comparisons with their paper plate. Help them to hold their scissors correctly. At this stage, they are quite likely to snip and tear, and this is fine. Look out for left-handers, who might just be noticeable at this age, and provide left-handed scissors.

Extension
Ask older children to look for squares as well as circles in the environment. What other shapes can they see? Talk about shapes that can roll, and experiment with any three-dimensional shapes that you find together.

HOME LINKS
Encourage the children to take their dinner plates home and tell their family that the plate is a *circle*. Ask parents and carers to help them find two more 'circles'.

MULTICULTURAL LINKS

Choose food magazines that represent a range of cuisine types for a multicultural feast!

GROUP SIZE
Four children.

TIMING
Five minutes.

UNDER AND OVER

Learning objective
To use words to describe simple positions.

What you need
A small table and chair; a box; a soft toy for each child; paper; pen.

Preparation
Put the table, chair and box on a carpeted area where the children can sit close by. Make a ticklist by writing the position words that you are going to use in one column and the children's names as headings for four other columns. Tick off the words that each child understands.

What to do
Invite each child to choose a toy to play this game with. Sit the children in a row facing the table, chair and box. Sit beside the children with your own teddy.

Explain that you are going to tell the teddies what they have to do. Tell your teddy to go '*on* the table'. Have your teddy make a few mistakes first. Place him *under* the table and ask the children, 'Is he *on* the table?'. Place him on the chair and ask, 'Is he on the *table*?'. Continue until Teddy has done it correctly. Suggest that the children's teddies show your teddy how to do it correctly. Now ask individual children to put their teddy *on* or *under* the *table* or *chair*. If the teddy makes a mistake, ask one of the other teddies to show her.

As the children become more accurate in carrying out the actions, introduce the box. This time the teddies can go *on* or *in* the box. In later sessions, introduce actions such as, 'Can your teddy *jump over* the table?', 'Can she *hide under* the table?'.

HOME LINKS
Ask parents and carers to find opportunities to practise these position words at home.

Support
Keep a careful note of the words that you are introducing and how many key words a child can understand at a time. This will provide valuable information for assessing a child's grasp of abstract vocabulary.

Extension
Use this approach to introduce other position words such as *beside, behind* and so on. Later, ask the teddies to show you which tower is *higher* or *lower*, or which plates of sweets have *more, less* or the *same number*. Keep a systematic record of each child's progress.

GROUP SIZE
Three or four
children.

TIMING
Ten minutes.

JUST RIGHT

Learning objective
To compare and match size.

What you need
A picture book of the traditional tale, 'Goldilocks and the Three Bears'; three bowls, three spoons, three chairs, three beds (shoe boxes adapt well) – each in a large, a middle and a tiny size; a doll (the same size as the baby bear) to play the part of Goldilocks; a baby bear, a middle-sized bear and a large bear.

What to do
Sit together with the children on a carpet. Show them the picture book of 'Goldilocks and the Three Bears'. Now bring out your props and introduce Goldilocks and the three bears to the children. Show them the chairs and ask the children to put the correct bear on the correct chair. Show them the bowls and spoons and invite them to put the correct-sized bowl in front of the correct bear. Finally, bring out the beds and again find the correct bear for each bed.

Start to tell your story once more. As you come to the part with Goldilocks trying the chairs, invite the children to select the large chair, the middle-sized chair and the tiny chair. Make Goldilocks try them out as in the story. Repeat with the bowls and use the spoons to give Goldilocks a taste of the porridge. Help the children to identify the large bed, the middle-sized bed and then the tiny bed. Finally, ask the children to help you act out the last part of the story by letting them each move a bear as you say the words.

Support
Let younger children hear the story a few times before you invite them to take part in the role-play. Save your props until a second or third session.

Extension
Ask older children to help you to find or make the different-sized props that you need.

HOME LINKS
Ask parents and carers to act out fairy stories with their children emphasizing size (such as *big* giant or *tiny* mouse).

MULTICULTURAL LINKS
Look out for stories from a variety of countries and cultures that can be used to reinforce the concepts that you are teaching. *The Singing Sack* complied by Helen East (A & C Black) has a good selection of stories and songs.

GROUP SIZE
Two or three children at a time.

TIMING
Five to ten minutes.

WATER TIME

Learning objective
To compare and play with quantities in the water tray.

What you need
Aprons; a water tray; a selection of transparent pouring objects such as plastic jars, bottles and tubs; food colouring.

Preparation
Add enough food colouring to make your water a dark colour. It will be easier for the children to see water levels as they pour, empty and compare. Ask the children to put on aprons.

What to do
Gather around the water tray and admire the colour of the water. See what the water looks like in the containers. Ask the children to choose a container and fill it up. Hold the containers up and ask, 'Who has more? Who has less? Pour out the water and fill it up again. Does this help to answer the question? Can you make your water the same as your friend's? Now try pouring your water into a larger container. Does it still look as much? Shall we put more in and fill it up? Can you empty that into the smaller bottle?'.

Continue questioning and experimenting so that the children can compare and learn about levels and quantities through their own actions. Listen carefully to what they are saying. This will give you an insight into their level of understanding. Continually reinforce the key words *more*, *less* and *same*.

Support
Younger children will need help with pouring and filling. Help by holding a funnel for them.

Extension
Encourage older children to investigate the quantities by themselves. They will be starting to understand that an amount of water stays the same whatever container it is put in. Set your older children challenges to make them think as deeply as they can about what is happening as a result of their actions.

HOME LINKS
Encourage parents and carers to play with their children in the sink or bath using different containers. Provide ideas for materials and activities in your newsletter or on your notice-board.

HOME LINKS
Give each child a
copy of the
photocopiable sheet
on page 75 to take
home. Ask parents
and carers to help
their child to colour
over the picture and
to count out the
candles. Suggest that
they encourage
their child to point
to the numbers in
turn as they count
'one, two, three'.

**MULTICULTURAL
LINKS**
Talk about birthday
celebrations and
how they are
celebrated in
different cultures.
Explain that Hindus
celebrate the
birthday of Lord
Rama; Christians
celebrate the
birthday of Jesus,
and Sikhs celebrate
Guru Nanak's
birthday.

BIRTHDAY CANDLES

Learning objective

To count and recognize sets and numbers to three.

What you need

Sheets of paper; stubby crayons; cards (approximately 20cm by 30cm) with the digits '1', '2' and '3'; a real cake with three (or more) candles or a model of a cake made from a cake tin covered in 'icing' with three (or more) candleholders glued onto it.

Preparation

Place the sheets of paper and drawing tools on a table.

What to do

When one of the children has a birthday, bring out the cake and celebrate with a song. Ask the child how old they are. Clap the number together several times so that everyone is used to chanting numbers as they clap, for example 'one, two, three'. Introduce the three number cards. Which number tells how old you are? Place the cards in the correct order and count them together. Ask how many candles there should be on the cake. Now invite three children to join you at a table. Give each child a sheet of paper and let them choose a crayon. Draw a 'cake' on each sheet of paper and show each child in turn how they can draw a vertical line from it to represent a candle. Count together as you draw three 'candles'.

Support

Talk with the children about what they are doing. Guide much younger children by holding your hand over theirs to help them draw the lines.

Extension

Encourage older children to draw up to five candles. Invite them to design you a beautiful cake on their sheet of paper.

GROUP SIZE
Three children.

TIMING
Five to ten minutes.

BIG AND LITTLE

Learning objective
To use simple words to describe size.

What you need
Ten pairs of objects which are identical in most respects, except for size, such as a big and a little brick, a big and a little box, a big and a little pebble; a tray.

Preparation
Arrange the objects randomly on the tray.

What to do
Show the children your tray of objects. Pick up a little brick and ask a child to give you the big one. Start with objects which are identical in every respect apart from their size, such as the bricks, and then move on to objects which are merely the same category, such as pebbles. After each turn, replace the objects before moving on to the next child. When each child has had three turns, repeat the activity, but this time pick up the big item and ask each child in turn to give you the little one. Again, let each child have three turns.

Now repeat the game but vary the question. Ask one child for a *little* object and the next for a *big* object. Finally, ask each child to respond to your directions alone, 'Can you give me the *little car*, please?' and so on. Make a note of any apparent difficulties so that you can reinforce the activity at another time.

Support
Start with just three sets of items and gradually build up the number.

Extension
Make the activity more difficult by providing sets of three objects such as a big, red brick; a big, blue brick and a small, red brick. Ask the children for more specific items such as, 'Can you pass me the *big, red brick*, please?'. Ask the children if they can think of any other words that mean *big* and *little*?

HOME LINKS
Invite parents and carers to contribute pairs of items for a dressing-up game such as a big and a little wellington boot, a big and a little hat, a big and a little cloak. Repeat the game with the dressing-up materials.

MULTICULTURAL LINKS
For bilingual children, make sure you know the corresponding 'big' and 'little' words in their first language so that you can teach the words in both languages.

GROUP SIZE
Two or three
children at a time.

TIMING
Five minutes.

JUMBLE SALE

Learning objective
To sort into very simple categories.

What you need
A box full of dressing-up clothes and materials. Provide distinct categories such as three or four bags, hats, pairs of shoes, skirts, jackets, shawls, shorts and so on (remove any items which might be ambiguous).

Preparation
Mix your collection of clothes together in a large washing basket or box. Place it in a position where the children can rummage through and spread out the clothes.

What to do
Tell the children that you need to sort out the clothes because you are going to have a pretend jumble sale, or you need to tidy up. Ask them to put all the dresses together in a pile, all the hats, all the shoes and so on. Start them off by putting one of each item at the bottom of a pile. Now, as far as possible, sit back and watch. Listen to the children's language as they discuss what they find and where it should go. Answer any of their questions and leave any 'mistakes' until the end. When they have finished, praise them warmly and go through each pile as you fold and bag the clothes. If any item is misplaced, simply ask all the children where they think this one should go, and they will think about it more closely.

HOME LINKS
Encourage parents
and carers to let
their children help
with sorting the
laundry by matching
socks together or
by putting all their
own clothes into
one pile.

Support
Start very young children with a simpler sorting task that they can manipulate and see more easily. Keep the choice smaller, for example sorting the toy cars from the trains or sorting two types of farm animals.

Extension
Help the children to sort the clothes to new criteria. Rucksacks could be sorted from handbags, or red dresses separated from blue.

**MULTICULTURAL
LINKS**
This game presents
a wonderful
opportunity to
explore a range of
multicultural
clothing and fabrics
together. Talk about
the colours and
textures and decide
together what
categories to sort
them into such as
yellows and reds;
shiny and not shiny;
silky and rough.

In this chapter you will find ten activities which encourage children's knowledge and understanding of their world. The children are given the opportunity to think about their homes, families and surroundings, as well as learning about how things move and work, and how to make simple models.

Knowledge and understanding of the world

GROUP SIZE
Three or four children.

TIMING
Five minutes.

HOMES AND FAMILIES

Learning objective
To talk about home and family.

What you need
Sets of farmyard animals such as cows and calves; horses and foals; sheep and lambs; pigs and piglets and so on; two large sheets of paper; felt-tipped pen.

What to do
Sit on the floor with the children gathered around you. Place one of the sheets of paper on the floor in front of you all and arrange the farmyard animals around the edge. Explain that the animals all

want to live in their families but have become muddled up. Can the children help? Talk together about where each animal lives, and let the children guide you with suggestions as you draw fields or sheds on your sheet of paper. Encourage the children to sort the animals into their families, placing each family into its home.

Now ask the children if they live in families too (be sensitive to all home circumstances). Lay out your second sheet of paper and talk with the children as you draw simple representations of their homes. Ask each child to tell you who lives in their home and draw simple figures to represent their families. Write each name beside the family member, using the children's words. Follow the children's ideas to add any distinguishing features to the homes, such as 'We live in the big flats'; 'We have a big tree' and so on.

Support
Encourage younger children to bring in a family photograph to make this activity easier for them.

Extension
Let older children draw their own family in the home you have drawn for them. Ask why families and homes are so important to us.

HOME LINKS
Ask parents and carers to look through family photographs with their child. Ask if the children may bring one in to show to the group.

MULTICULTURAL LINKS
Talk about families and homes celebrating cultural variations. Talk about the children's other family members who might not live close by.

HOW I FOUND MY WAY

Learning objective
To talk about the recent past.

What to do
Gather the children around and talk about how they came to the group that session. Ask, 'Who walked? Who came in a car? Who came in a pushchair? Who came on a bus? Who did you travel with? How will you get home again?'.

Now sing the song below together (to the tune of 'Here We Go Round the Mulberry Bush'). As you come to each verse, add an individual line for each child and encourage everybody to mime walking, pushing a pushchair, driving a car, sitting on a bus and so on.
  When I came to play today
  This is how I found my way
  (add an individual line)
  All the way to see you!
For the individual line, make up something special for each child such as, 'Nana brought me in the car'; 'I walked with Mummy all the way'; 'Sitting on the bus today' and so on.
  Now talk about their journey to the group that day. Ask, 'What was the weather like? What do you remember seeing? Did anyone else see that too? Who helped you cross over the road? Where did you catch the bus or park the car? Did you meet anyone else on your journey?'. Encourage the children to remember and talk about the things that they saw or heard along the way.

Support
Ask parents or carers who bring in younger children to tell you how they travelled to the group so that you can remind the younger ones about their journeys.

Extension
Work individually with the older children and use their recollections to help you draw a simple map of their journey on a long sheet of paper. Include the sites and events that the children tell you about.

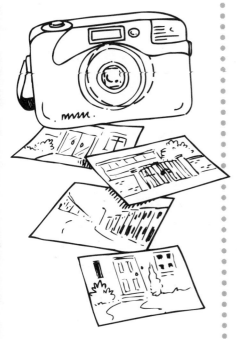

PHOTOGRAPH GALLERY

Learning objective
To examine and talk about photographs of the locality.

What you need
A set of photographs of your locality and the inside and outside of your setting.

Preparation
Take six or seven photographs of local landmarks such as the town centre, the local mosque and the playground. Take another three or four of the views which the children will see as they arrive at your setting – the pathway to your door, the outside of your building, your front door. Take a further twelve or so of your play area, showing different activities or the equipment that is out each session. Add some photographs of individual significance for your children such as their homes and their corner of the village. When these are developed and sorted, you will be ready to start this activity.

What to do
Gather the children around you on the carpet. Tell them that you have some photographs to show them. Start with the photographs of the general locality, including any views of where individual children live. Do the children recognize any of the photographs? Talk about where the photographs are from and encourage the children to share ideas.

Now show the children the views of the outside of your setting. Do they recognize the views? Ask them to help you to put them in order, representing what you see first and what you see next as you come to the group.

Finally, spread out your views of the play area. What can the children see? Encourage each child to choose one of the photographs and find that part of your room. Continue until everyone has had two or three turns.

Support
Ensure that younger children have a helping partner as they try to match the photographs to the different parts of the room.

Extension
Older children love to be part of your preparation – ask them to help you as you choose photographs to take inside your setting.

GROUP SIZE
Two or three children.

TIMING
Five minutes.

HOME LINKS
Ask parents and carers to help their children gather more precious things together. Ask them to go for a walk around their neighbourhood or the local park, helping their child to collect natural objects of interest. Ask them to bring the objects to the group to show and to talk about.

MULTICULTURAL LINKS
Try to collect natural objects from around the globe – an exotic feather, a piece of soapstone, a stick of spice, a cotton ball. Talk about where each one came from.

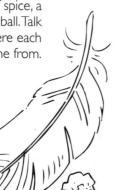

PRECIOUS THINGS

Learning objective

To collect, handle and think about natural objects.

What you need

A collection of natural objects in a box such as a beautiful shell, a fine feather, a mineral rock with crystals or metallic specks, an interesting pebble, a pine cone, a piece of natural sponge, a dried seed head (such as 'Japanese lantern'), a flower, a twisted twig.

What to do

Sit down comfortably on the floor. Tell the children that you have found some precious things to show them. Bring one object at a time out of the box and show it to the children. Show them how to handle the object carefully and to pass it to each other. Talk about how it feels, what it looks like, whether it has a smell or a sound. Ask the children if they know what it is and talk together about where it came from. Do the children think that this precious thing was made by a machine? Introduce the word 'nature'. Start a 'nature' table so that the children can handle and talk about the things you collect there.

Support

Show younger children how to handle the objects gently and carefully. Talk to them about the objects as you encourage them to handle them and feel the textures.

Extension

Provide older children with a selection of obviously manufactured items (coloured plastic toys, crayons and so on) and natural objects and ask them to sort them into 'made' or 'natural'. Ask them to tell you why they have chosen to sort each one in a particular way.

RAINY DAYS AND SUNSHINE

Learning objective
To observe the weather and record it in a simple form.

What you need
A large sheet of paper with a box drawn for each session that week; paints and pens; a set of blank sticky labels to fit in the boxes that you have ruled.

Preparation
Use a dark pen to draw suns, clouds, rain or snow on your sticky labels, depending on your current weather conditions.

What to do
Gather a few children at a time to help you to prepare your weather chart. Help them to paint sunshine and rain blobs around the border, and ask them to colour over the stickers that you have drawn. As you work together, tell them that you are going to be talking about the weather this week. Ask, 'What is the weather like today?'.

Mount your chart on the wall, and gather everyone together. Show them the decorated chart and explain that you are going to use it to show what the weather is like each day. Go outside, or stand by a window, and decide what you are going to record today. Ask, 'Is the sun shining? Are there lots of clouds? Is it raining? Is it frosty or snowy? Are the leaves blowing about?'. Choose a sticker together to represent the day's weather and mount it on the chart.

Support
Limit the choice to sunshine or rain, leaving the chart blank when these do not apply.

Extension
Ask older children to record the variations of the wind as well. Create a second set of stickers for a strong wind, a gentle wind or no wind at all and agree together how to depict these on your stickers.

	Morning	Afternoon
Monday	☀	☁
Tuesday	☁	🌧
Wednesday	☀	
Thursday		
Friday		

JUNK FACTORY

Learning objective

To choose from a selection of materials to make a 'machine'.

What you need

A collection of 'junk' material such as cardboard boxes, yoghurt pots, chocolate boxes, wrapping material, corks, bottle tops, plastic containers, foil paper; pots of paste; pastebrushes; a picture book or selection of magazines with pictures of machinery.

Preparation

Arrange the junk materials on a low surface so that the children can see what is there.

What to do

Gather all of the children together and show them the pictures of the machines. Talk about what each machine does and point out any interesting parts – the big wheels for carrying heavy loads; the cutters for cutting the corn; the big hammer for beating the metal flat. Encourage the children to share experiences about machines that they have seen working. Talk about machines in the home, such as the vacuum cleaner or the washing machine. Keep the ideas simple and explain that machines have been made by people to do jobs for us.

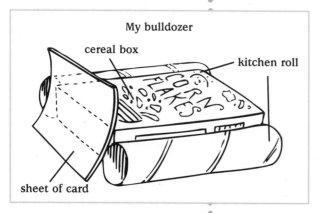

My bulldozer

cereal box

kitchen roll

sheet of card

Now encourage the children to think of a machine that they would like to invent. What job will it do? What will it look like?

Work with two children at a time and help them to choose the junk material they would like to use to make their machine. When they tell you what they would like to make, provide ideas but let them decide. For example they might choose to make a bulldozer out of a large cereal box, a card sheet and two kitchen rolls (see diagram). Show them how to use the paste to stick the sections together. As you work, talk about what the machine will do and what all the parts might be for.

Support

Encourage younger children to think of a job that they would like their machine to do, and help them to choose suitable materials to make it. Use hand-over-hand to assist with sticking if necessary.

Extension

Let older children paint their models. Help them to add one or two moving parts, such as wheels that turn or a crane that has string to lift it.

GROUP SIZE
Three or four
children.

TIMING
Five minutes.

HOME LINKS
Ask parents and
carers to help their
child to find three
things around their
home which move
by wheels. Ask them
to draw these,
asking their child to
add the wheels. This
will help the child to
remember them.
Invite the children
to bring their
drawings in to share
with the group.

INVENTING THE WHEEL

Learning objective
To explore movement and talk simply about how things work.

What you need
Ideally, you need large, soft-play foam pieces such as cylinders, blocks, cubes, balls, flat sections. If these are not available, you can make a table-top version of this activity by using wooden blocks and cubes, cylinders or cotton reels, large round beads and flat sections. Add a square of carpet on your table-top to give it surface friction.

Preparation
Place the cylinders and any rounded shapes on one side.

What to do
Gather the children around the soft-play pieces or table-top. Suggest that you try making a car together. Show them the flat section and suggest that the people could travel on that. How can the children make it move? What does it need? Experiment together as you try raising the flat section onto the blocks or cubes. See how difficult it is to move. Encourage the children to talk about how they could make their car better. As they suggest adding wheels, ask them how you could make wheels for your car. Encourage them to look for suitable pieces to use, including the rounded shapes that you have placed to one side. Experiment together to see which shapes work best. Encourage the children to use the correct vocabulary, talk about *round* shapes that *turn* and help the car to *move*.

Support
Younger children will enjoy using the large soft-play pieces and seeing whether they can move each other on their 'car'. Show them a selection of toy vehicles and help them find the wheels and turn them *round*.

Extension
Challenge older children to design cars out of junk material with rounded wheels attached by split-pins.

GROUP SIZE
Six children.

TIMING
Ten minutes.

TOWERING HIGH

Learning objective
To build towers and simple constructions.

What you need
Six large stacking (not interlocking) blocks (10cm x 10cm x 10cm) such as painted lightweight polystyrene blocks, shoe boxes covered with bright paper or light blocks from large construction kits; six medium stacking blocks (5cm x 5cm x 5cm); six small stacking cubes (1cm x 1cm x 1cm), cushions or carpet squares; a low table.

What to do
Arrange the cushions or carpet squares in a circle on a smooth floor and invite the children to sit down. Show them how you can stack a high tower in the middle of the circle using the largest building blocks. Now give each child one block and take it in turns around the circle to add a block to the tower. See whether you can stack all the blocks before they fall down. Have three or four turns, starting in a different position around the circle each time. Now bring out the medium blocks and again take turns around the circle to add a block to make a tower. Next, move to stand around your low table. Repeat the activity with the small cubes, encouraging very careful finger movements as new cubes are added to the tower. The children may only manage to build a tower of two or three bricks high now. Praise all their attempts and have fun knocking down the towers at the end.

Support
Ensure that the youngest children place their blocks first or second so that they do not have to balance them too high. Demonstrate the action for the children and help them by gently placing your hands over theirs, if necessary.

Extension
Leave a selection of stacking blocks out for the older children to build and stack safely. Use a variety of shapes, including cylinders that can only be stacked if placed end-on.

HOME LINKS
Ask parents of younger children to help them practise stacking boxes or bricks on top of each other at home. Suggest that they gradually build the number up to four or five.

GROUP SIZE
Three children.

TIMING
Ten minutes.

HOME LINKS
Ask parents and carers to look for the chance to take their child to a railway station, or go on a train journey.

MULTICULTURAL LINKS
End the journey by calling out 'goodbye' in as many languages as you can. Invite children who speak another language to tell the others how to say goodbye in their language.

ON THE TRAIN

Learning objective
To talk about train journeys.

What you need
A picture book about trains (any of the *Thomas the Tank Engine* books by Rev W Awdry or Christopher Awdry would be favourites); three child-sized chairs and one for yourself; a whistle or flag; dressing-up clothes; snacks.

Preparation
Arrange the four chairs one behind the other in the style of a train.

What to do
Look through the picture book together and ask the children if they have been on a train before. Ask, 'What was it like?'.

Explain to the children that you are going on a pretend train journey together. Ask, 'Where would you like to go? What do you need to do?'. Spend time in your dressing-up corner, choosing clothes to wear and packing up bags. Ask, 'What else might you need?'. Pack a simple snack such as a wrapped biscuit or a drink.

Now pretend that you are going to the station. The train is waiting for you! Decide who is going to be the guard at the back of the 'train' and take first turn at being the driver yourself. Ask the guard to wave the flag or blow the whistle when all the passengers are sitting down safely.

As you travel, comment on all the things you pretend to see. Encourage the children to join and to imagine the journey with you. When the 'train' reaches your destination, stop for a 'picnic'.

On the way home, allow other children to take turns to be the driver and the guard. Sing a song, such as an adapted version of 'The Wheels on the Bus', as you travel 'home'. Ask the children to add ideas for the verses.

Support
Arrange the 'train' seats in pairs so that an adult can sit next to a younger child and encourage them to join in with the game.

Extension
Develop the game into an extended role-play, with the children directing the ideas and you encouraging and supporting them.

GROUP SIZE
Two or three children.

TIMING
Ten minutes.

JUMPING JACK

Learning objective
To make a simple moving stick puppet.

What you need
A jack-in-the-box; the photocopiable sheet on page 77; card; sticky tape; scissors (for adult use); washable felt-tipped pens; lightweight sticks or dowelling (5mm in diameter and 30cm long); small screens or boxes.

Preparation
Make a copy of the photocopiable sheet for each child. Mount each sheet onto card and cut around the outline. Arrange all your craft materials on a table.

What to do
Give each child a jack-in-the-box shape and encourage them to add colour with felt-tipped pens. Most of the older children will be able to stay approximately within the lines; the younger children will scribble freely and this is appropriate at this stage.

Show the children your real jack-in-the-box and how it springs up out of the box. If you have little children who may be frightened of the noise or the sudden movement, make sure they are familiar with the toy before surprising them with it. Explain that you are all going to try to move your own puppets like a jack-in-the-box.

Help the children to attach the end of a stick to the back of their puppet using sticky tape. Show each child individually how to hold and work their puppet. Demonstrate how to make it 'jump' up from behind a box or a screen.

Support
Younger children may find it easier to paint over their puppet using broad brushstrokes of colour.

Extension
Help older children to make a box for their 'Jack'. Have the stick emerging through the base of a cardboard box the same height as the puppet. Show the children how to make their puppet hide by pulling the stick downwards, and how to make it jump up by pushing the stick upward through the hole. Encourage them to think and talk about how to solve the practical problems they are faced with when they try to make their model move.

HOME LINKS
Ask parents and carers to encourage their children to give them a simple puppet show at home.

This chapter has ten activities for helping young children to develop their physical skills. There are activities to encourage confidence and control in both large and fine physical movements, from balancing and climbing to rolling and shaping dough. There are games to help the children think about position and space and to enjoy joining in with movement.

Physical development

GROUP SIZE
Four children.

TIMING
Ten minutes.

HOME LINKS
Encourage the children to borrow a plastic skittle and sponge ball to take home so that they can practise their rolling and aiming.

TO AND FRO

Learning objective
To roll a ball with an approximate aim.

What you need
A large sponge ball to roll (approximately 15cm diameter); a smooth surface to sit on; an additional adult helper.

What to do
Sit on the floor together in a circle. The adults should sit opposite each other, with two children each side of them. Sit with your legs splayed in a V-shape in front of you so that the six of you are making a six-point star shape with your legs. You should be spaced so that your toes almost touch.

Roll the ball to your helper who should return it. Now begin to roll the ball to the children. The position of their legs means that they are virtually guaranteed to catch the ball. For a while, enjoy rolling and returning the ball to each other without asking the children to aim it to anyone in particular. Praise and encourage the children as they aim and catch. Now suggest that each child rolls it to another who you have named and pointed to. This time, the children will have to aim more carefully.

Now let them have a turn in telling you who they are going to roll it to, calling out the other child's name as they push the ball away. Let every child have a couple of turns of rolling and catching in this way. Finally, enlarge your circle a little so that everyone has to aim more carefully and roll the ball over a slightly longer distance. Again, encourage them to call out a child's name before they aim the ball to them.

Support
If you need to, place very young children in front of you so that you can help with the aiming and catching.

Extension
Practise your aiming and rolling by playing a skittles game together.

GROUP SIZE
Three or four children.

TIMING
Ten minutes.

BALANCING ACT

Learning objective
To develop balance in a safe environment.

What you need
A large space, indoors or out, which is safe to move on in bare feet or plimsolls/trainers; a collection of safety mats and non-slip carpet squares or door mats (ensure that the mats will not slip on your surface as the children jump onto them); aluminium foil; scissors (for adult use).

Preparation
Lay the mats out across your floor so that each one is within 15cm of another. Cut out twelve fish shapes from the foil, about 10cm long. Place these to one side.

What to do
Encourage the children to take off their shoes and socks and go barefoot (or wear plimsolls) for this activity. Show the children how to move across the mats, pretending that they are stepping-stones across the water. Ask them to try to move carefully, balancing so that they do not step into the 'water' (the floor). Praise their efforts and move the mats slightly further away from each other. Encourage the children to balance and move safely as they continue to avoid the 'water'.

Now place the fish about 10cm away from different 'stepping-stones'. Challenge the children to pick them up by balancing carefully on their mat and stooping, still without stepping into the 'water'. Celebrate your 'catch' together.

Finish by putting the mats together to sit on and sing the nursery rhyme, 'One, Two, Three, Four, Five, Once I Caught a Fish Alive'.

HOME LINKS
Ask parents and carers to help their child practise balancing on one leg for one or two seconds. Can they try for even longer?

Support
Make sure the distances which younger children have to balance or reach across are just wide enough to be challenging, yet close enough for the children to be successful.

Extension
Draw chalk lines to balance along, heel to toe.

ROCKING AND ROLLING

Learning objective
To develop balance and control during an action song.

What you need
A carpeted area to sit on; a washing-up bowl part-filled with water; a toy boat; the song on the photocopiable sheet on page 71.

Preparation
Learn the words and actions to the song 'Little boat' given on the photocopiable sheet.

What to do
Kneel down in a circle on the carpet together. Put your boat on the water and show the children how it floats. What will happen when there are waves? Show how the boat will *bob* up and down. Now pretend the waves are stronger, and make the boat *rock*. Finally, show how the boat will *roll* from side to side as the waves get even stronger.

Put your bowl of water to one side and invite the children to sing the boat song with you. As you sing the first verse, bob gently up and down from a sitting position. Can the children rock from side to side without using hands for the second verse? Rock widely from side to side for the third verse, using your hands to steady yourselves. Finish with the first verse again as you all bob calmly. The song is sung to the tune of 'Bobby Shaftoe's Gone to Sea'.

Support
Hold younger children around their waists to help them rock and roll, encouraging them to use a supporting hand when they need to. This activity is an excellent way for very young children to develop trunk support and 'saving' reactions from a sitting position.

Extension
Invite older children to practise the movements to the verses of the song in a standing position as well.

SHIP AHOY!

Learning objective
To use the climbing frame with developing skill and imagination.

What you need
A climbing frame with safety mats beneath; a flag; pirate hats (see diagram); kitchen roll tubes (as spyglasses); a large sheet; other props chosen by the children from your home corner; a pirate picture book such as *Captain Teachum's Buried Treasure* by Peter Carter and Korky Paul (Oxford University Press). If the children are still unsteady when climbing, you will need one-to-one adult supervision.

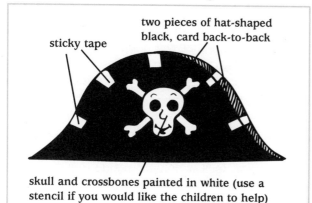

sticky tape

two pieces of hat-shaped black, card back-to-back

skull and crossbones painted in white (use a stencil if you would like the children to help)

Preparation
Set up your climbing frame so that it is a safe height for your youngest children. As a rule, any platform or top rung should be at about a child's chest height. Arrange your safety matting underneath (or ensure that there is safety surfacing underneath an outdoor frame).

What to do
Sit together in your book corner as you look through the pirate picture book. Show the pirates in their hats, looking out to sea with their spyglasses as they try to see other ships coming. Can the children see a pirate flag? Let each child choose a pirate hat.

Move on to your climbing frame and pretend that it is a pirate ship. Support the children as they climb up the 'ship' and help them to balance with one hand as they wave a flag or look through a spyglass. Talk to the children imaginatively as they play.

Now pretend that it is night-time and the pirates need somewhere to sleep. Help the children to choose props from the home corner to arrange under the frame, making a tent with the sheet. The next 'morning', when the pirates wake up, 'clear the decks' (remove your props out of the way) and practise climbing up the frame once more.

Support
You will need to judge just how much support your younger children need as they climb. Help any children who are timid to place one foot on the first rung as they wave their flag or look through their spyglass.

Extension
Develop this game into a longer imaginative role-play. Help older children to climb higher on the frame as their balance and awareness of safety improves.

GROUP SIZE
Two children at a time.

TIMING
Five minutes.

GIANT FOOTSTEPS

Learning objective
To move with confidence and developing imagination.

What you need
Vinyl (waterproof) paint; an outdoor surface for painting footsteps on, or alternatively, use a long strip of polyethylene sheeting to lay on an outdoor surface or hall floor; one large and one child-size pair of old shoes; a 'surprise' such as a giant teddy bear or a huge boot.

Preparation
This activity is most fun when you have an outdoor playground or path that you can paint on permanently. Paint at a time when the area can remain undisturbed until it is dry. Cover the soles of the old shoes with paint and print a trail of ten 'giant' footprints (approximately 15cm apart). Continue the trail with ten small footprints. Alternate these with more giant prints, ending with the small prints side by side as if the walker is jumping 'feet together' several times. End with the two large footprints side by side as if the 'giant' has jumped into the air and disappeared. Use your imagination and whatever space you have to make the trail as interesting and as varied as possible. Hide a surprise boot or giant teddy at the end of the trail.

What to do
Encourage the children to follow the trail, making giant steps to match the giant prints, and small steps to match the small prints. Practise jumping together as you come to the jumping steps. Can the children place their footsteps exactly over the footprints? Talk about *big* steps and *little* steps as you go and enjoy the surprise at the end. Reassure the children that the giant is 'just pretend' if you need to!

Support
Hold younger children's hands as they try to balance and to jump. Gradually remove your support as they become more skilled.

Extension
Help the children to make their own footprints with washable paints and sheets of paper.

HOME LINKS
Suggest that parents and carers help their child to practise taking big and little steps, counting as they go.

GROUP SIZE
Three children.

TIMING
Five minutes.

BEANIE BAGS

Learning objective
To move and to throw with increasing control.

What you need
A coloured beanbag for each child and one for yourself; six safety mats; a large floor area. This activity works best if there are two adults.

Preparation
Arrange the safety mats so that they form a circle of 'stepping-stones', with a gap of about half a metre between them.

What to do
Ask the children to watch you as you show them what to do. Stand on the first mat and throw your beanbag onto the second mat. If you miss the mat, go and fetch the beanbag and have another turn. As soon as your beanbag lands on the mat, pick it up and aim at the next mat. Continue like this until you have gone all around the circle. Now invite the children to try, one child at a time. Encourage everybody to cheer as the beanbag lands on the next mat. Praise the other two children for watching, waiting well and cheering.

When everyone has had a turn, encourage the whole 'team' to move around the mats together. Let all three children throw their bag onto the first mat. When everybody's bags have landed, throw them to the second mat. Proceed around the mats as a team, only moving on to the next mat when all three children's bags have 'landed'. Again, encourage the children to cheer and support each other, and keep the children's attention through your enthusiasm and encouragement.

Support
Move around the mats with younger children, helping them to throw with an approximate aim.

Extension
Move the mats slightly further apart to challenge older children to aim and throw further.

HOME LINKS
Suggest a simple aiming game for parents and carers to play with their children, such as throwing a beanie toy into a basket.

GROUP SIZE
Whole group, up to a maximum of 20 children.

TIMING
Five minutes.

HOME LINKS
Use tissue paper to make simple origami shapes such as a flower or a boat (see diagram). Encourage the children to carry them home without crushing them.

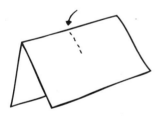
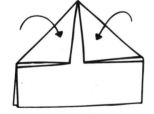
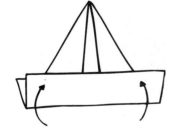

GENTLE TOUCH

Learning objective
To handle delicate objects with care and control.

What you need
A long strip of soft tissue paper (a new roll of soft toilet tissue is ideal); a carpeted area to sit on; an adult or older helper to every two children; coloured pens.

Preparation
With the coloured pens, draw a smiling snake's head on the end of your paper roll and draw colourful zigzag lines down the length of it. By the end of the activity, your 'snake' needs to be long enough to go twice around your circle of children and adults, allowing for any breaks.

What to do
This activity is bound to raise a few giggles, but is an excellent way of encouraging gentle fingers. Sit down in a circle together on the carpet. Have one adult sitting between every two children, so that adults and children are evenly spaced out.

Tell the children that you are going to pass around a paper snake! Can they can pass it to the next child so that it does not break or tear? They will have to do it very *slowly*, and very *gently*. Unravel the roll of paper carefully (you will have to unravel quite a bit so that you always have slack). Encourage the child next to you to take the end of the snake from you and pass it very gently to the next child as you feed out the paper.

How far can you pass the paper snake around the circle before it breaks? Keep the activity fun and celebrate all successes. If it breaks, draw on a new 'head' and start the paper roll again in a different place around the circle so that everyone has a few turns.

Support
Keep the number of children in the circle small when you have younger ones. If possible, alternate an adult with each child so that the children can be helped to pass the paper snake carefully and gently around the circle.

Extension
Help older children to make twisted streamers using long strips of tissue paper or crêpe paper. Remind them to handle the paper gently and carefully so that it does not tear.

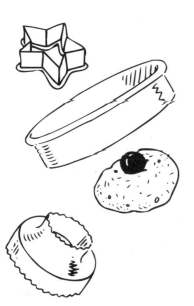

BAKER'S SHOP

Learning objective
To shape and roll dough.

What you need
Ingredients to make play dough (the recipe is on the photocopiable sheet on page 78) in different colours, but mainly yellow; rolling pins; spatulas; plastic knives; shape cutters; paper plates; a table; play money; baskets.

Preparation
Make up the play dough and put out small quantities with the baking implements.

What to do
Encourage the children to join you at the baking table as you show them how to roll sausage shapes and balls out of the play dough. With your help, these can easily become 'buns' (with a small ball on top to represent the cherry), sausage rolls (surround one colour with another, roll it into a long sausage and then cut into sections), turnovers, loaves and French sticks. Now show the children how to roll the dough flat to make tarts and biscuits using the cutters and your imaginations!

Tell the children that you would like to make a baker's shop to play in and help the children to arrange their baking neatly onto paper plates. When everyone has had a turn, arrange the plates of food on a table to form a 'shop'. Play alongside the children as you hand money to the 'shop assistant' and choose which cakes and bread you would like to buy. Take turns to be the shop assistant and the shopper.

Support
Show younger children how to roll a ball and a sausage by moving your hand gently over theirs. Withdraw your hand as they begin to manage by themselves.

Extension
Suggest that older children invent sweets for a sweet shop, or make fruit and vegetables for a greengrocer's.

WRIGGLY WORMS

Learning objective
To creep and crawl through a series of obstacles.

What you need
Early years 'sacks' for the children to jump or crawl in (see Preparation for suggestions); a non-slip surface to move on such as a carpet or safety mats outdoors; a selection of safe obstacles to crawl around.

Preparation
You can make an early years version of the traditional 'sack' by using old pillowcases and strongly sewing a handle onto each side for the child to hold. Tough fabric and strapping also works well. The sacks should come up to the children's waist height. Make a simple obstacle course – a plastic tunnel if you have one, a large cardboard box to climb through, some giant scatter cushions to clamber over, beanbag chairs to climb between and loose net curtains to wriggle underneath.

What to do
Show the children how to move and crawl safely in their sacks. Let them pretend that they are wriggly worms and encourage them to move through your obstacle course safely and with enjoyment. Emphasize key words as they crawl *under*, *over*, *through* and *between* the obstacles. Help them to finish the obstacle course by standing up and shuffling slowly to the end with their feet inside their sacks.

When you have all reached the end of the course, sing this song together (to the tune of 'Row, Row, Row Your Boat') before wriggling back 'home' through the obstacles again:

Wriggly, jiggly, wriggly worms,
Crawling through the ground,
Wriggly, jiggly, wriggly worms,
Never make a sound!

Support
Stay close to young children and hold a hand, if you need to, whenever they stand up in their 'sacks'.

Extension
Encourage older children to rearrange the obstacles and make it as difficult as they can.

GROUP SIZE
Three or four children.

TIMING
Five to ten minutes.

HOME LINKS
Ask parents and carers to look out for wide spaces in the neighbourhood as they travel home with their child. Where can they see green spaces? Where are there lots of buildings?

SPACING OUT

Learning objective
To develop an increasing awareness of space and of others.

What you need
A hoop for each child (one that the children can stand inside and be able to hold on each side); a large floor space; a cassette player and a musical cassette to dance to; an additional adult to operate the music.

Preparation
Set up your cassette ready to play.

What to do
Take the children into a hall or open space. Give them the hoops to play with for a minute. Show the children how to step inside a hoop and hold it around them by placing a hand on each side of it. Suddenly they are *wider*. Show them how much space they have around them now. Encourage them to stride around holding their hoops around them.

Help the children to walk past each other without bumping into one another. When they hear the music, encourage them to dance carefully around the room, avoiding each other. Explain that when they hear the music stop, they should put their hoops down in a space and sit in the middle of them. Help the children to look for wide spaces and to spread themselves out over the floor. Start and stop the music several times.

When the children have got used to spreading out, ask them to move around without their hoops and still find a big space to sit in when the music stops.

Support
Lead younger children by the hand yourself, or arrange for older children to partner them.

Extension
See whether older children can organize themselves into a circle, spacing themselves out. Show them how they can do this by joining hands, stepping apart, and then sitting down.

The ten activities in this chapter aim to encourage young children's creative development. The ideas span from model-making and collage to dance and music-making. Children are encouraged in this chapter to respond confidently and creatively to what they see, feel, hear, touch and smell.

Creative development

GROUP SIZE
Four to six children.

TIMING
Five minutes.

SOUND EFFECTS

Learning objective
To respond in a variety of ways to what is heard.

What you need
A tambourine; a drum; a swanee whistle (or similar).

What to do
Help the children to sit in a circle on the carpet. Bring out the tambourine. When they hear it shake, can they wobble all over? Show them how to do this, and have two or three turns. Encourage each child to watch you and beat the tambourine sharply as you stop, encouraging all the children to stop still. Always do the actions with them to provide a model and to encourage confidence.

Now bring out the drum. Can they clap their hands when they hear the drum? They may not be able to do this to a set rhythm yet and this is appropriate at this stage. Alternate the drum with the tambourine for a few turns. Can the children remember to wobble or to clap? Keep the activity fun and share their laughter as they do this. When they are secure, introduce the swanee whistle. Can the children stand *up* as the sound goes *up* and sit *down* when it comes *down* again? Practise for a few turns, exaggerating the movement as you sweep your hands *up* and *down*. At a later session, begin to play all three sounds one after the other so that the children have to listen to the sound and decide which action to perform.

Support
Spend the first few sessions just working with one sound and action before you begin to combine them.

Extension
Arrange for an additional adult helper. Stand where the children cannot see you and play the sounds. Can the children still carry out the actions, just by listening to the sounds alone? Encourage the children to make up some more actions to go with the sounds.

HOME LINKS
Ask parents and carers to help their child to identify three sounds that they can hear at home. Invite the children to remember and tell you about them.

MULTICULTURAL LINKS
Introduce some instruments from a variety of countries for this game; a rainmaker, castanets and a selection of guiros and shakers. Ask the children to think of some actions to make that would go with these new sounds.

SKYSCRAPERS

Learning objective
To explore large model making in three dimensions.

What you need
A picture book or photographs of skyscrapers, including views at night-time; dark blue and black sugar paper; staple gun; scissors, yellow sticky paper; a selection of large cardboard boxes; paste; pastebrushes; black paint; thick paintbrushes.

Preparation
Session 1: Mount sheets of dark blue sugar paper on the wall (from skirting board to child's height) to make a frieze. Cut out 'skyscrapers' from black sugar paper and mount these over the blue paper. Make sure that there is an open space in front of the frieze.

Session 2: Arrange cardboard boxes, paste and pastebrushes on a low table.

Session 3: Make up some pots of black paint.

What to do
In the first session, look at the photographs of skyscrapers with the children. Talk about the people who live or work there. Ask the children what they think it might be like to live in a skyscraper. Admire how the windows in the tall towers look bright against the dark sky.

Suggest to the children that you make your own picture of skyscrapers. Show the children your frieze and cut out oblongs of yellow sticky paper for them to stick on as 'windows'. Take a few seconds to look at the effect of this together.

In the next session, invite the children to make their own models of skyscrapers. Show them how to choose the cardboard boxes to stack and help the children to paste them together to make a tall shape. Leave these to dry.

During the third session, paint the models of the skyscrapers black, with the children, and place them in front of your skyline frieze to make a three-dimensional display.

Support
Give younger children extra broad brushes for pasting and painting and work alongside them to show them what to do.

Extension
Ask older children to add windows and lights made of yellow sticky squares to their models.

GROUP SIZE
Two children at a time.

TIMING
Five minutes.

SAND BETWEEN THE TOES

Learning objective
To respond in a variety of ways to the sense of touch.

What you need
Holiday photographs of the seaside, including the beach; a shallow tray (a large seed tray is ideal); dry play sand; pouring beaker; two nursery chairs; a soft towel.

Preparation
Half-fill the tray with sand. Place it on the floor with a chair at each end.

What to do
This activity is for the sheer indulgence of experiencing sand between the toes and talking about how it feels! Show the children the holiday photographs and ask them if they have ever been to the seaside. Talk about the sandy beach, how you can play there and how it feels to walk across it. Show the children your sand tray and together try to imagine a whole beach of sand.

Ask two children to sit down on the chairs and help them to remove their shoes and socks. Invite them to touch the sand with their toes. What does it feel like? Can they wiggle their toes? Does it feel smooth or rough? Gently use your beaker to pour sand over their feet as you talk together. Bury their feet and encourage them to feel gently for each other's toes under the sand. Can they find them again? Smooth over the surface and see if they can each make a clear footprint. Can they make patterns with their toes?

When you have finished, clear the sand gently from between the children's toes with a soft towel and help them to put their shoes and socks on again.

HOME LINKS
Suggest a walk through crunchy snow, or a stride through fallen leaves. Can parents and carers help their children to find words to talk about what it feels like?

Support
Let younger children watch at first. Encourage them to explore the sand with their hands before trying with their toes.

Extension
Make up some other trays to feel with toes – dried beans (not red kidney), rice, small pebbles (ensure that younger children don't swallow small particles). Encourage the children to express what they feel.

One group tried jelly to the children's great pleasure and found that this provided an excellent stimulation for language!

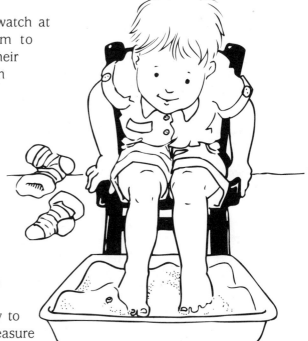

GROUP SIZE
Two or three children.

TIMING
Five minutes.

MAKING WAVES

Learning objective
To explore colour and texture in two dimensions.

What you need
Paints in different shades of blues and greens; real combs or thick cardboard; scissors; blue sugar paper; overalls; paintbrushes.

Preparation
Make up some thick paint by adding a small amount of water to powder paint, or by adding a thickener such as wallpaper paste. Cut combs out of cardboard (to make different patterns when drawn across the thickened paint). Arrange the paints, brushes and combs on a low table.

What to do
Help the children to put on overalls and encourage them to paint over a sheet of sugar paper with broad brushstrokes. Encourage them to mix the colours so that they have a mass of blues and greens on their paper. Suggest that they apply the paint thickly. When they have covered the paper, use your own brush to smooth over the surface slightly in order to spread the paint evenly. Now show the children how the combs draw the thickened paint into lines. Help them to use the combs to make wavy patterns all over the paper. Place the wave pictures somewhere horizontal to dry thoroughly.

Support
Before the activity spend a short time showing younger children how to draw waves on the surface of the sand tray, guiding their fingers gently with your hand.

Extension
These paintings are beautiful as they are, but older children might like to make them into a landscape picture. Suggest that they paint a small boat to cut out and stick on top of the dried waves.

HOME LINKS
Encourage parents and carers to take their children along to the local art gallery or sculpture park to admire and talk about the shapes and colours there.

MULTICULTURAL LINKS
Look for examples of wavy patterns in fabrics and pottery from around the world and see if you can trace over them with your fingers.

GROUP SIZE
Two children at a time.

TIMING
Ten minutes.

TOUCH PICTURES

Learning objective
To explore textures and touch.

What you need
A3-size thin card; paste; pastebrushes; collage materials (small shapes of fine and course sandpaper, small pieces of textured fabrics, sections of sequinned fabric and tinselled fringe/braid, a selection of buttons, small pieces of shiny card); a tray.

Preparation
Arrange your craft materials on a low table. Spread the collage pieces out on a tray so that the children can easily select items.

What to do
Show the children your collage pieces and enjoy feeling and looking at them together. Talk about the textures using words such as *rough*, *smooth*, *scratchy* and *bumpy*. Suggest that the children make a feely picture. Help the children to paint a piece of card with paste so that it is sticky all over. Now encourage them to choose one piece of collage material at a time and press it onto their paste. Can they find interesting pieces which all feel different? Encourage them to place rough next to smooth so that you have interesting contrasts in texture. Continue until the whole card is covered with collage materials. Place the pictures somewhere horizontal to dry.

When they are dry, talk with each child about what their picture looks like – the colours, the shiny shapes, the way the pieces are placed next to each other. Now encourage them to close their eyes and touch the surface of their picture gently. What can they feel? Arrange the collages on a display table and encourage the children to feel each other's pictures with their fingertips.

Support
Provide larger collage pieces to make the task shorter and the pieces easier to handle.

Extension
Involve older children in the choosing and cutting up of suitable craft materials so that they are planning their collage ahead.

HOME LINKS
Suggest that parents and carers do a bark rubbing with their child by placing a sheet of tracing paper over a rough tree and scribbling over it with a wax crayon. Encourage them to talk together about how the tree bark feels.

MULTICULTURAL LINKS
Choose some brightly coloured ethnic fabric to back your design area. Use it as a stimulus for selecting collage materials. Discuss the colours, textures and patterns.

GROUP SIZE
Two children at a
time.

TIMING
Ten minutes.

GLITTER PRINTS

Learning objective

To explore colour and light through handprints and footprints.

What you need

Paint trays; paint; glitter; wash bowls; towels; large sheets of paper; an additional adult helper.

Preparation

Make up some thick paint and add enough glitter to make all the paint glittery. Lay your paper on the floor beside the paint tray. Place a wash bowl and towel close by.

HOME LINKS
A glittery handprint
or footprint makes
a very personal
greetings card for
families to 'keep
forever'. Copy the
photocopiable sheet
on page 79 onto
thin card for each
child and help them
to make a handprint
in the appropriate
place. Together, fill in
the missing words
on the card and let
each child give their
card to their
families. Ask parents
and carers to keep
the cards safe.
Repeat the activity
every term and ask
parents to talk with
their child about
how they are
growing.

What to do

This activity will work best if you are prepared to show the children first! Remove shoes and socks, place one foot firmly into the paint tray, and make a firm footprint onto your paper. Wash and dry your foot, and repeat with a handprint.

Now encourage the children to take a turn, helping each child to place their foot and hand firmly into the paint and onto the paper. Ask your helper to assist with removing shoes and socks, washing and drying feet and hands, and putting shoes on again.

Gradually build up your picture as more children add their prints. This activity makes a wonderful wall frieze if you vary the colours of the paint and glitter. Place it where the light will catch the glitter. Admire it with all the children and talk about the colours, the different sizes and the way the glitter sparkles in the light. It is also special because it was made by all of you together.

Support

Begin with just the handprints for very young children.

Extension

Encourage older children to enjoy using several of their prints to make patterns and designs on the sheet of paper.

DANCING DAY

Learning objective
To respond to music with dance and movement.

What you need
A box of props including coloured chiffon scarves, ribbons, floating shawls; cassette recorder; blank cassette; an open space or hall.

Preparation
Make up your dance tape in advance. You will need about 30 seconds of five different types of music, all suitable for dancing to. Begin with a modern release, then a section of ballet music such as Tchaikovsky's *Swan Lake*, some rhythmic or mechanical music such as Mike Oldfield's *Tubular Bells*, some ethnic or folk dance music such as African drums, *River Dance* by Bill Whelan, or some Scottish country dance music.

Finish with a dramatic section from a musical such as *Jellicle Ball* from *Cats* by Andrew Lloyd Webber.

What to do
Move into your open space and encourage the children to enjoy dancing to the music. Place the props on the floor and take out items to add to the effect – a scarf to hold above you as you move, a shawl to form 'wings' as you 'fly' and a large feather to wave. Encourage the adults to move in an uninhibited way, providing ideas for the children to copy until they have relaxed into the activity. Play the tape through once. The second time, pause the tape in each section and talk about the music. How does it make you want to move? Share ideas – a mechanical robot, a flying bird or a striding giant. Praise the children for moving in new and interesting ways. Play the tape a third time and encourage the children to put their ideas into practice.

Support
Let younger children dance with one of the adults.

Extension
Let older children help you to select pieces of music for your next tape.

LOOK AND SEE

Learning objective
To respond in a variety of ways to what is seen.

What you need
A selection of small boxes – wooden boxes, decorative gift boxes (with lids that open easily), painted matchboxes, jewellery boxes; a selection of interesting items to go inside – a shell, a bracelet, a little doll, a toy car, a piece of shiny rock, an old button, a coin.

Preparation
Arrange the selection of boxes on a low table and place one 'treasure' inside each of them.

What to do
Invite the children to come to the table and explore the boxes carefully. Show them how to lift the lids or turn the tops in order to open them. Praise them for handling the boxes carefully and gently. Share the surprise as you find the 'treasure' and talk about each one. Hide each treasure carefully again for the next child to find. When everyone has had a look, challenge the children to remember which box had which treasure. Ask, 'Can you remember where the shell is? Where did we hide the car?'. Move the boxes around so that they are arranged in a different order. Can the children still find the correct box? Look and see if they are correct.

Support
Make sure that the boxes are easy to open, the treasures are not too small, and the selection is limited to three.

Extension
Invite older children to choose a selection of treasures and put them into the boxes each session. The children will begin to explore the boxes themselves and be interested to discover what they can 'look and see' that session.

GROUP SIZE
Six children.

TIMING
Five minutes.

SPECIAL SMELLS

Learning objective

To respond in a variety of ways to the sense of smell.

What you need

Four plastic transparent containers; 24 cotton-wool balls; a selection of four liquids that have distinctive and pleasant odours (such as perfume, orange juice, diluted tomato sauce, drinking chocolate).

Preparation

Prepare this activity immediately before you do it. Dip cotton-wool balls into each of the four liquids so that they have taken up the smell but are not dripping. You will need six cotton-wool balls for each odour (one of each odour per child). Place the scented cotton-wool balls in the four containers, one per odour.

What to do

Gather the children around and talk about different smells. Invite the children to think of familiar smells. Ask, 'Who likes that smell? Do all things smell nice? What is your favourite smell?'. Now pass around the first jar and invite each child to take a cotton-wool ball and smell it. (Ensure that they do not try to taste it and be aware of any allergies to perfumes.) Tell the children what the smells are first. Ask, 'Do you like that smell? Have you smelled it before?'. Talk about each of the four smells in turn. Make sure that the children wash their hands after carrying out the activity.

HOME LINKS
Tell parents and carers that you have been thinking and talking about smells in your group. Encourage them to talk to their children about familiar smells at home, particularly at mealtimes?

Support

Younger children might be wary of smelling new things. Give them the cotton-wool ball to hold so that they can control how much of it they smell. Spend time before this activity exploring smells in your group – sniff the apple juice and the orange juice, smell a newly-cleaned wash area and sniff the outside air. Help the children to make links between noses and smelling.

Extension

Encourage older children to match a sauce bottle, a bottle of perfume, a tin of drinking chocolate and a carton of juice to each of their four cotton-wool balls. Some of the children might even be able to guess what the smells are without any visual clues.

GROUP SIZE
Whole group
(children and
adults).

TIMING
Ten minutes.

BAND TIME

Learning objective
To explore making musical sounds together.

What you need
A cassette recorder; a selection of tapes or a helper who plays the guitar or keyboard; a large cover or cloth; a selection of percussion instruments – shakers, drums, bells, scratchy guiros, tambourines; the children's home-made instruments made from plastic containers with dry pulses in, sealed with strong glue to keep the contents secure.

Preparation
Arrange the instruments on a low table, covering them with a cloth until you are ready to carry out the activity.

What to do
Gather everybody in a circle, sitting on the floor. Ask two or three children at a time to choose an instrument and bring it back to the circle. The children will probably not be able to sit quietly – as soon as they have their instrument they will wish to experiment with it. This is appropriate at this stage.

When everyone has an instrument, play the musical accompaniment for a few seconds. Stop the music suddenly. As you do so, move quickly around the inside of the circle, engaging eye contact with everyone and holding your finger to your mouth in a 'ssh!' sound. Praise everyone for stopping. Tell the children to play again when they hear the music and to stop playing when it stops. Have two or three turns, keeping the musical interludes to about ten seconds.

Now stand up with your instruments and encourage the children to follow you in a 'Pied Piper' procession all around the room. Continue to start and stop as the music does. From time to time let the children experiment with a new instrument. The last time you march around the room, encourage the children to replace their instruments on the table as they pass it.

HOME LINKS
Give each child a copy of the photocopiable sheet on page 80 to take home, showing ideas for making musical instruments.

MULTICULTURAL LINKS
Try your library's school loan scheme or the local education authority's music department to see whether you can borrow a selection of multicultural percussion instruments.

Support
Lead younger children in your procession and show them how to make sounds with their instrument.

Extension
Encourage older children to lead the band as you march around the room.

A letter to Grandma

'Oh dear,' said Mum. 'Grandma's had to go into hospital. She has to stay for two weeks.'

'Can we phone her?' asked Sophie.

'Not really,' said Mum. 'But we could go and see her on Wednesday.'

'But she won't know we're going,' said Sophie.

'We'll send her a letter to tell her,' Mum said. 'Besides, she'll be very pleased to hear from us. You could draw her a picture.'

Out came the paper and pencils and the envelopes and the stamps. Mum did the writing. Sophie did the thinking. 'What should we put?' Mum asked.

Sophie thought hard. 'Start with Dear Grandma,' she said. 'And say that on Wednesday Mum and Sophie will come to see you.' Then she added, 'We could take some flowers. And some grapes.'

'So we could,' said Mum.

'Tell her to get better quickly,' said Sophie, watching carefully as Mum wrote the words. 'And tell her I will bring my Charlie Bear for her to cuddle in bed.' She thought hard again. 'Put love from Mummy and Sophie, and do lots of kisses at the bottom.'

Mum said, 'You could do the kisses yourself.'

So Sophie did. Then, on another piece of paper, she drew a picture of Grandma in her hospital bed, with Charlie Bear tucked up beside her, a big bunch of flowers on her cupboard, and Mum and Sophie sitting on her bed.

'Where are the grapes?' Mum asked.

'We've eaten them all up,' said Sophie.

Carefully, they folded the letter and the picture into an envelope. Mum wrote the address on the front. Sophie stuck down the envelope then licked the stamp and stuck it onto the front. Off they went, to the post-box around the corner. Sophie stood on her tiptoes to push the letter into the box.

On Wednesday, Mum and Sophie stood at the bus stop with Charlie Bear, a big bunch of flowers and a brown paper bag full of grapes.

When they arrived at the hospital, Grandma was sitting up in her bed, waiting for them.

'Well!' she said, 'I'm so pleased to see you!'

'Did you get our letter?' asked Sophie, excitedly.

'Of course I did,' said Grandma, smiling. She opened her cupboard drawer and took out the letter and the picture. 'It came yesterday,' she said, 'and I've read it one hundred and fifty six times so far. It cheered me up no end!'

Sophie glowed. She was pleased the letter had cheered Grandma up.

'We'd better eat up all the grapes now,' said Sophie. 'Then the letter and the picture will be true!'

And everybody laughed as they tucked in.

© Irene Yates

One, two, three, look at me!

One, two, three,   *(clap hands three times to the 'one, two, three')*
Look at me!   *(point to yourself)*
I am counting,   *(clap hands three times to the 'one, two, three')*
One, two, three!

Say 'hello'!   *(shout out 'hello!')*
Turn around,   *(everybody turn in a circle)*
Stamp your feet   *(stamp three times to the rhythm)*
And touch the ground.   *(reach to the floor)*

Clap your hands,   *(clap hands three times to the rhythm)*
Reach them high,   *(hold your hands up high)*
Shut them tight,   *(shut your hands up tightly)*
Then wave 'goodbye'.   *(then finish with a big wave)*

© Hannah Mortimer

Take this home and teach it to your family.

Little boat

Little boat is sitting on the water,
Little boat is sitting on the water,
Little boat is sitting on the water,
   Bobbing up and down like this.

Bobbing up and down like this,
Bobbing up and down like this,
Bobbing up and down like this,
   Sailing on the sea.

Little boat is rocking on the water,
Little boat is rocking on the water,
Little boat is rocking on the water,
   Rocking side to side like this.

Rocking side to side like this,
Rocking side to side like this,
Rocking side to side like this,
   Sailing on the sea.

Little boat is rolling on the water,
Little boat is rolling on the water,
Little boat is rolling on the water,
   Rolling all around like this.

Rolling all around like this,
Rolling all around like this,
Rolling all around like this,
   Sailing on the sea!

© Hannah Mortimer

Sing this song together, as your child sits on your knee. The tune is 'Bobby Shaftoe's Gone to Sea'. As you sing, encourage your child to:
■ keep looking at you
■ keep their balance as you move them
■ anticipate what is coming next
■ have fun!

_____ has done it 'All by myself!'

Planning ahead

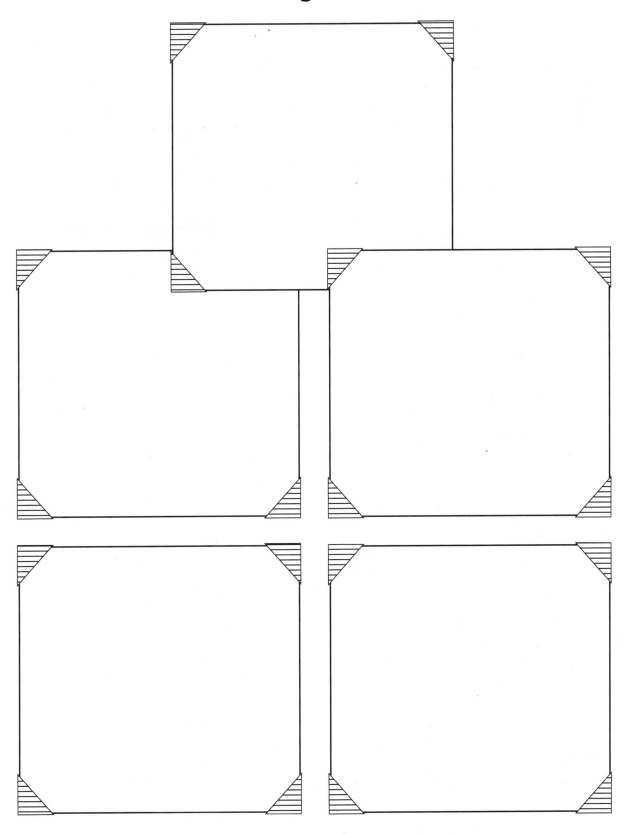

These are all the things that I chose to do first!

Puppet play

Here are some ideas to try at home.

■ Make a simple puppet theatre for your child.

■ Ask your child to tell the puppet a story by looking through a picture book together.

■ Make a simple glove puppet out of an old sock!

■ Encourage your child to talk on a toy telephone to the puppet.

Puppets are an excellent way of encouraging imaginative play.

Birthday candles

Count the candles

Rainy days and sunshine

What is the weather like today?

Monday

Tuesday

Wednesday

Thursday

Friday

Saturday

Sunday

Colour over a sun, some rain or a cloud, so that you can remember.

Jumping Jack

Making play dough

Make up some play dough with your child. Ask them if they can make an interesting shape to take into their group.

You will need
2 cups of plain flour
1 cup of salt
4 tablespoons of cream of tartar
2 cups of water
2 tablespoons of cooking oil
food colouring (optional)

  a saucepan
  a wooden spoon
  a board
  a plastic box or bag

Instructions
1. Put everything into a pan and mix it together. Your child can help with this part, too.
2. Cook over a low heat for five minutes, stirring all the time.
3. Knead the dough on a floured board while it is still warm.
4. Divide the dough into sections and add a different food colouring to each batch, kneading it in.
5. Store in a plastic box or bag in a fridge or cool place.

Glitter prints

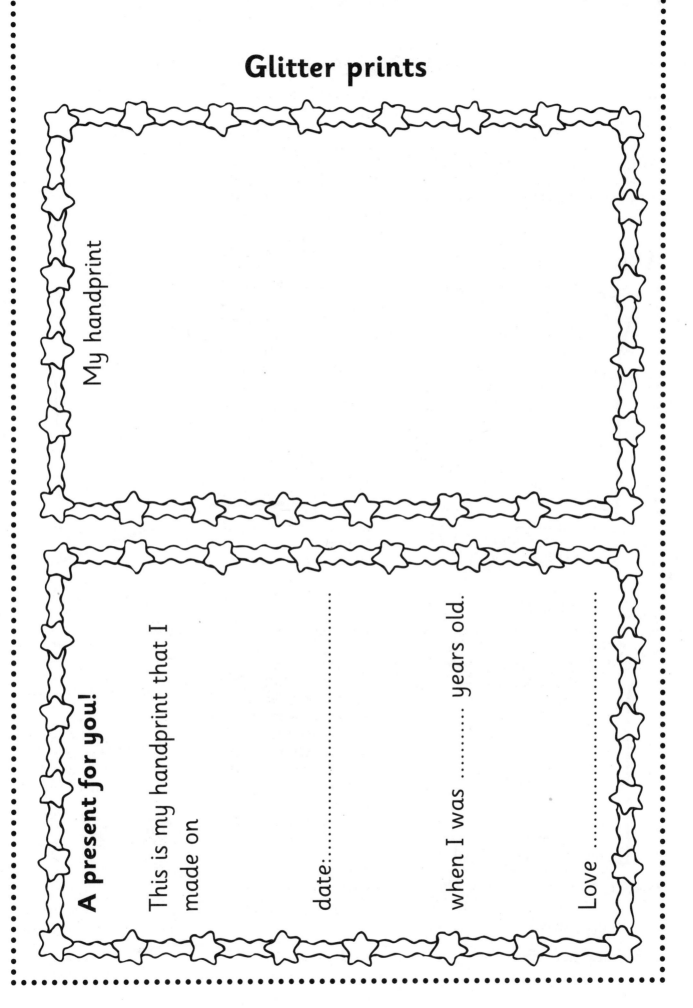

My handprint

A present for you!

This is my handprint that I made on

date:...

when I was .... years old.

Love ....

Band time

Have fun making these musical instruments at home!

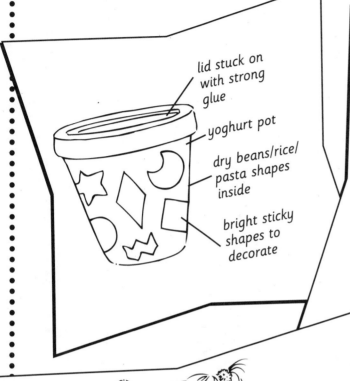

lid stuck on with strong glue

yoghurt pot

dry beans/rice/pasta shapes inside

bright sticky shapes to decorate

lid stuck on with strong glue

dry beans/rice/pasta shapes inside

bright sticky shapes to decorate

Saucepan lids make wonderful cymbals.

Pans, buckets and strong bottles all make super drum kits with wooden spoons and spatulas.